SIX PERSPECTIVES ON NEW RELIGIONS: A CASE STUDY APPROACH

SIX PERSPECTIVES
ON NEW RELIGIONS:
A CASE STUDY APPROACH

BY

ANSON D. SHUPE, Jr.

STUDIES IN RELIGION AND SOCIETY
VOLUME ONE

THE EDWIN MELLEN PRESS
NEW YORK AND TORONTO

Library of Congress Cataloging in Publication Data

Main entry under title:

Six perspectives on new religions.

　　(Studies in religion and society series; v. 1)
　　Bibliography: p.
　　1. Cults--North America--History.　2. Religions--
History.　3. North America--Religion.　I. Shupe, Anson D.
II. Series: Studies in religion and society series
(Edwin Mellen Press) ; v. 1.
BL2520.S55　　291'.0973　　　81-9464
ISBN 0-88946-333-6 (cloth)　AACR2
ISBN 0-88946-983-0 (hard)

Studies in Religion and Society　ISBN 0-88946-863-X

Printed in the United States of America

For my wife,

Janet Ann

CONTENTS

INTRODUCTION

Two basic generalizations may be made with confidence about the religious impulse: first, it is uniquely human; and second, it appears to be wellnigh universal, rooted (as the early French sociologist Emile Durkheim noted) in the needs of every community and social group. By the same token, religious change and innovation are as natural and inevitable a set of processes as the existence of religious belief itself. To have norms and customs, Durkheim observed, is to insure deviance, and it is the same with religious change and the history of religions. This book was inspired by the particular religious ferment taking place during the late 1960s, the 1970s, and the 1980s in North American society. However, as readers will quickly see, it is by no means limited to those groups. Indeed, to scholars and students of American religion it should be patently obvious that the type of religion which I shall refer to as "fringe" has been a familiar feature in western culture. The religious innovations of the last half of the twentieth century simply chance to be the ones which first caught and held my interest.

I approach the study of fringe religions as a sociologist. However, because many readers and users of this text may not share this orientation, I have deliberately avoided whenever possible the overuse of social science jargon and needless neologisms. This book is a survey of points of view in the most literal sense, and its interdisciplinary thrust is meant to inform as broad a

readership as possible. My general purpose is to provide readers with a sense of the various alternative
perspectives and assumptions currently used by scholars
and professionals to study fringe religions.

Several additional comments may be of benefit not
only to interested persons and students who simply want
to expand their understanding of and sensitivity to
fringe religions but also to instructors working from
this text. First, the histories of individual religious
movements, sects and cults are staggering in number.
Sociologists and others have charted their regularities
and continuities. However, a complete review of that
larger body of historical research would require enormous effort and space. As a result, I pragmatically restrict myself here to categorizing and analyzing recently published studies of fringe religions and generally
delete consideration of the mammoth historical literature, though I consider the historical--and one classic
example of historical research--as the sixth perspective.
This emphasis on more recent eras may have some advantage since groups emerging earlier in western and oriental history are likely to be less familiar to readers.

Second, many readers may be aware that the controversy over "new religions" in North America and Europe
of the 1970s and 1980s prompted a loosely organized
backlash movement which aimed at severely maiming, if
not actually wiping out, many recent fringe religions
(again, hardly an original wrinkle on the face of inter-
necine warfare conducted between religious groups in
western history). The burgeoning literature on this
"anti-cult" movement requires a separate lengthy analysis (as I have helped try to give it elsewhere--readers
are encouraged to consult Shupe and Bromley, 1980;
Shupe, Bromley and Oliver, Forthcoming), but the repression of fringe religions is not our subject here--except

as it may touch on the Criminological Perspective (see "Interpretations of Fringe Religions").

Third, concerning the format of each chapter, I originally intended to include whole articles and/or extended excerpts of studies that exemplify each of the perspectives discussed here so that readers could judge more easily for themselves the congruence between my classificatory claims and actual writings. This became impractical, as I wished to present relatively lengthy works such as Martin's The Kingdom of the Cults and other monographs. Hence, I have drawn up only abstracts of the illustrative research, but I hope readers will become interested enough to obtain the original work and formulate their own appraisals. Furthermore, the serious interdisciplinary analysis of fringe religions on such crucial issues as conversion and apostasy is still rather basic (if not downright primitive), and there are many aspects of these groups yet only dimly understood. Therefore, each chapter concludes not only with suggestions for further reading but also with what I have determined to be unresolved issues and topics for further investigation. Readers may weigh these in their own minds and hopefully sensitize their own awareness of the complexity of researching religious faith. Instructors can use them as departures for fruitful class discussions and more open-ended speculation.

Fourth, I believe that the fringe religions that compose the subject of this book possess a fascination value that we as informed voyeurs should not, in our struggle to appear dispassionate, deny. We are not, after all, concerned here with varieties of humdrum, established middle-class Protestantism. Religious innovation can often be located on the cutting edge of social process, social revolution, and cultural evolution.

Therefore, I do not apologize for the sensational examples of religious innovation presented in the pages to
follow nor for my repeated attempts to maintain a sense
of novelty and wonder about them. All religions, even
the strangest, consistently ask the truly meaningful
questions about human existence and order.

Lastly, I wish to thank several persons who directly or indirectly helped with this project. Lois
Williams, as usual, aided the manuscript production with
persistence and reliability. My departmental chairman,
Eugene Ramsey, provided me with a work schedule ideally
suited to a compulsive writer's needs. My long-time
friend, anthropologist Akira Yamamoto, though he may not
realize it, began my serious interest in religious movements when he introduced me to the new religions of
Japan as a graduate student, and I acknowledge now that
invaluable exposure. Herbert Richardson showed a good
deal of faith in first encouraging me to undertake this
project, for which I am grateful. Finally, as will become apparent to readers of my previous work, I bear an
intellectual debt to David G. Bromley, a co-author and
friend who has infused my own thinking on religious
movements with greater theoretical sensitivity.

REFERENCES

Shupe, Jr., Anson D. and David G. Bromley. 1980. The
    New Vigilantes: Deprogrammers, Anti-Cultists and
    the New Religions. Beverley Hills, CA: Sage.
Shupe, Jr., Anson D., David G. Bromley, and Donna
    Oliver. Forthcoming. The American Anti-Cult Move-
    ment: A Bibliographic History. New York: Garland
    Press.

INTERPRETATIONS OF FRINGE RELIGIONS

Human ingenuity, applied to religion, can produce some pretty queer things. Consider, for example, this vignette: A healthy, intelligent young man in his early twenties, with several years of college and perhaps a fiancee or girlfriend as well as a job, hears the teachings of a Korean named Sun Myung Moon at a combination dinner/lecture to which he was invited by another innocuous youth. The lectures essentially portray the present as a unique time to restore or establish the actual Kingdom of God on earth (a task, he learns, that Jesus Christ was unfortunately prevented from completing when he was prematurely crucified). Upon joining the Moon movement, the young man has to forsake his former associations and ties (school, job, girlfriend, friends) since he is required to work full time to recruit more members and/or fund-raise at shopping centers and airports. Since the opportune time to bring about the Kingdom of God will not last indefinitely, he will be encouraged to drive himself as hard as possible, even giving up such amenities as regular meals and more than a modicum of sleep. As his full energies are poured into group activities, inevitably his self-identity will begin to change. He may even change his name and adopt a Biblical alternative, such as Jacob or Joshua. He learns quickly to treat all women as his sisters (just as he regards all men as his brothers) and lives in uncompromising celibacy. If he wore long hair (or even

1

stylishly cut hair) and a mustache or a beard when he joined, he will trim the former and shave off the latter. He will not smoke, drink alcohol, or take drugs. He will believe that a middle-aged Korean man who can barely stumble through a sentence in `broken English, through Divine Revelation, now understands the true hidden meaning of the Bible better than all previous interpretations, scholars and theologians. When this Korean guru decides that the time is opportune, the young man may be married (in a mass ceremony of hundreds or thousands of movement members) to a woman (black, white or oriental) he has likely never before met, and after the wedding ceremony he will observe at least a fortyday period of sexual abstinence. To make matters more severe, upon joining he may even have signed a pledge stating that he is willing to go to South Korea to die for the movement if necessary. Should his biological parents oppose his participation, he may define them as "Satanic" and even cease all but the most sporadic communication with them.

Aside from objections that this description of a "Moonie" convert is something of a caricature, readers may not see its individual elements as all that bizarre. After all, Catholic women who enter some present-day religious orders have their names changed, their heads shaved, and their individuality deliberately stamped out by uniforms and humbling exercises (e.g., long hours of praying, meditating, chanting, fasting, foot washing). They also experience lives of uncompromising celibacy as brides of Christ, sometimes virtually cut off from families except for infrequent prearranged visits. Some orders take vows of silence; others forbid the wearing of shoes to demonstrate their devotion and piety. Thus, perhaps it could be argued that the "Moonie" example

above is not really so out of the ordinary in American
religion and not nearly as "queer" as I presented it as
first.[1]

Therefore, consider these additional curiosities:
In the chaotic years immediately following Japan's de-
feat in World War II, Japanese society suddenly saw the
birth and spread of hundreds of new religions, some
merely variations on traditional beliefs and others totally without precedent. Out of this ferment came one
incredible group calling itself Denshin-kyo (literally,
"religion of electricity") which reportedly worshipped
electricity, as manifested in the light bulb, as the supreme form of deity and considered Thomas A. Edison as a
lesser god or prophet in its pantheon (Schiffer, 1955).
About the same time South Korea was experiencing similar
postwar social upheaval that likewise witnessed the rise
of a number of unusual religious groups. One particular
movement, the Park Chang No Kyo (Olive Tree Movement)
was led by an ex-Presbyterian named Park who was reportedly held in godlike reverence by his almost two million
followers. They believed him to be a shaman whose mere
touch could bestow healing benefits. As a result, they
believed that physical ailments could be cured by drinking Park's bathwater and also water with which he washed
his feet (Moos, 1964). Closer to home, a cult know as
the Body, which roamed throughout the United States during the late 1970s and 1980s, was nicknamed the Garbage
Eaters due to its repulsive custom of refusing to eat
anything that its members did not obtain through forag-
ing expeditions into the waste bins outside restaurants
and supermarkets. The Body believed itself an elect
group that alone would be saved in an imminent confla-
gration that would consume the world. It justified its
culinary obsession by reference to Luke 16: 19-31 and

the example of the poor man Lazarus who fed on the
scraps of the rich man's table but after death resided
with Abraham in heaven while the rich man suffered in
hell. Finally, the following classic anecdote of self-
mutilation and masochism recently came to my attention
through a local newspaper:

> KUALA LUMPUR, Malaysia (AP) A West German
> businessman has completed his conversion to the
> Hindu faith by piercing himself through the
> cheeks with a ¼ inch thick, 4 foot-long steel
> rod and pulling a chariot for two miles by
> ropes attached to his back and chest with
> steel hooks. The man, who identified himself
> only as Ray, completed the Hindu vows Monday
> by pulling the chariot through the streets of
> Seremban City to the Maha Mariamman Temple
> where the hooks and steel rods were removed.
> Ray--who prefers to be called by his Hindu
> name of Ganeson, or Elephant God--said he de-
> cided to convert after meeting a Hindu man
> identified as A.K. Sundram, five years ago.
> . . . Ray took part in the annual Aadi festi-
> val, a time when Hindus traditionally thank
> their God for giving them insight into life.
> Aadi is the fifth month of the Hindu lunar
> calendar and Monday was the day of that month
> set aside for a ritual affirmation of faith.
> Many Malaysian Hindus take part in the cere-
> mony. After days of fasting, the faithful are
> skewered with steel rods, hooks, needles,
> pins, and other sharp instruments. Others
> walk through 20 foot-long pits of fire, don
> shoes with soles made of nails, or hang
> spreadeagled in the air from hooks embedded in

their backs. The worshipers chant songs which they say put them into trances through which they feel no pain. (<u>Fort</u> <u>Worth</u> <u>Star</u> <u>Telegram</u>, 8/12/80)

When reading reports of people lacerating their bodies, drinking each other's bathwater, eating garbage, praying to electrical circuits, one is tempted to conclude that they were insane or (charitably giving them the benefit of the doubt) seriously misled. Or were they? What taken-for-granted assumptions do we or any observers conceal in such off-hand judgments, and from what perspectives (defined as highly organized sets of assumptions) are such judgments made? What would those believers say of Christians in ritualistic cannibalistic fashion drinking wine (or grape juice) and eating wafers as they explicitly acknowledge these to be the analogues of the flesh and blood of Jesus Christ? Or nuns wearing wedding rings to signify their devotion and unconsummated betrothal to a dead man?

These sensational preliminary examples are intended to do more than merely pique the reader's interest in the subject of fringe religions. They illustrate the heterogeneity of religious faith and challenge us to examine introspectively our own reactions to others' passionately held beliefs. Before considering the matter of how we interpret such religions, however, I want to identify their substantive domain and explain why I refer to them as "fringe."

FRINGE RELIGIONS DEFINED

Sociologists and theologians customarily draw a rough, common sense distinction between mainline religious groups and all others that do not fit their conception of what it is to be mainline. Mainline Protestant

denominations such as the varieties of Methodism, Con-
gregationalism, Presbyterianism, and Lutheranism, for
example, are large, wealthy, middle to upper class in
their membership composition, and "established" (e.g.,
well over a century or more old). They are comfortable
in society, having made their peace with the secular
world. Missionaries of mainline churches restrict their
activities to Asians and Africans or to equally foreign
sub-populations of their own society (such as inner-city
derelicts, illegal aliens, and convicts in prison). As
if by gentlemen's agreement, they do not aggressively
try to poach members from one another's congregations.
Indeed, why should they? Particularly among some Protestant groups there is an uniformity in church services,
prayers, hymns and other details that, without much ex-
aggeration, almost makes these denominations interchangeable. The Roman Catholic Church is also mainline
as are the several largest forms of Judaism. While obviously not all these groups are interchangeable, various
authors (e.g., Kennedy, 1951; Herberg, 1960) have argued
that there exists in the United States at least a three-
pronged mainstream coalition or "triple melting pot" composed of these Protestant, Catholic and Jewish organizations that has tacitly agreed to live and let live.

On the other hand, non-mainline groups present a
problem of classification about which there is less
agreement. The question of how to identify and sort out
nonmainline groups continues to present an unresolved
problem for scholars of religion. Some groups are now
in the transition process of leaving their nonmainline
group status and entering the mainline classification
(for example, the upwardly socially mobile Southern Baptists). Others can only approach mainline respectability but still not achieve it (for example, the Church of
Jesus Christ of the Latter Day Saints or the Christian

Scientists) for doctrinal reasons or because of other sectarian characteristics. They are almost, but not quite, acceptable for membership in the fraternity of mainline groups.

Further down the continuum past the mainliners and quasi-mainliners, however, are those groups that--whatever their pretensions--are clearly unconventional, culturally deviant, and generally uncomfortable with some aspects of society as it is. These are groups such as the Theosophists, the Unification Church, the Black Muslims, the Hare Krishna movement, the Children of God, and our colorful Garbage Eaters described above. To the extent that their differences from mainline groups are blatant and sharp, society (largely composed of persons with mainline Judeo-Christian religious backgrounds) responds with pejorative labels for these groups. Labelled as such, they come to inhabit the fringe of public respectability. FRINGE RELIGIONS ARE ALL THOSE GROUPS NOT ACCORDED FULL SOCIAL RESPECTABILITY NOR RECOGNIZED AS BEING OF EQUAL STATUS WITH THOSE RELIGIOUS GROUPS IN WHICH MOST AND/OR IMPORTANT SOCIETAL SPOKESPERSONS PARTICIPATE AND WITH WHICH THEY IDENTIFY. Social respectability is a matter of degree, as I have indicated, and the fringe religions with which we will be concerned here have the least of it. I prefer the term "fringe" to describe in the broadest possible terms these unconventional groups because no alternative single term adequately encompasses all nonmainline groups. Readers may be familiar with the term "cult" and wonder why I do not simply label all groups cults. After all, don't the two terms--fringe and cult--mean the same thing? The term "cult" is a good example of the terminological inadequacy for such groups that I mentioned earlier and deserves a brief digression to illustrate this point.

"Cult" has become a popular "buzzword" during the
past few years as parents in the 1970s came to use it to
refer to the wide variety of fringe religions and movements of which they disapproved but in which their adult
offspring unfortunately participated. The media picked
up on the term undoubtedly because of its vaguely exotic, unsavory connotation. The parents' anti-cult
movement, however, eventually ran the term into the
ground, applying it without discretion. Anti-cultists
lumped together not only recent controversial groups
such as the Unification Church, the Hare Krishnas, and
Scientology, but also older sectarian groups such as
the Jehovah's Witnesses and less controversial evangelical organizations such as those operated by Billy
Graham, Oral Roberts, and Herbert and Garner Ted Armstrong. They then proceeded to throw in nonreligious
organizations, movements and fads such as EST (Erhard
Seminar Training), yoga and meditation, and even kung fu
and aikido schools in their obsession to root out and
expose "mind control".[2] In large part the blame for anti-cultists' indiscriminate overuse of the term "cult"
can be laid at the feet of various sympathetic evangelical Christian writers who have traditionally designated
as cults various groups whose doctrines did not closely
overlap with their own standards of Christian orthodoxy.
Walter Martin's The Kingdom of the Cults (1977) foisted
the "cult" label on Mormons, Jehovah's Witnesses, Christian Scientists, Spiritualists, Zen Buddhists, and Ba-
hais, among others, irrespective of these groups' dif-
fering affinities to Judeo-Christian tradition, their
sizes, longevities, and so forth. (Martin is discussed
at length in "The Philosophical Perspective.")

At the same time sociologists have grappled with
defining and elaborating the term "cult" so as to make

it less arbitrary. Their definitions can be generalized
as "cultural", "structural", or "mixed". Those prefer-
ring a cultural distinction, i.e., based on the group's
belief content, reveal the influence of the older anthropological use of the term "cult", meaning a set of beliefs and rituals centered around the worship of some
supernatural entity. Glock and Stark (1965: 245), for
example, locate cults as possessing theologically alien,
deviant beliefs. Lofland (1966: 1) identifies cults
by their theological tendency to "espouse very different
views of the real, the possible and the moral." Dohrman
(1958: xi), prior to either Lofland or Glock and Stark,
also used cultural criteria to define cults. He wrote:

> The concept of "cult" will refer to that
> group, secular, religious, or both that has
> deviated from what our American Society con-
> siders normative forms of religion, economics,
> or politics, and has substituted a new and of-
> ten unique view of the individual, his world,
> and how this world may be attained.

There are problems with such purely cultural definitions since they obviously assume that there is agreement or consensus (reread Lofland's definition) on what
is mainline religion and that a given "cult" can be
shown clearly and reliably to vary from this established
norm. However, no accompanying criteria for mainline
normalcy are ever presented in these cultural definitions. Mainline consensus remains either an unverified
or an unexamined assumption.[3] This is not to say that
most persons in a society do not share certain "core"
beliefs and assumptions; rather, cultural definitions
leave the domain and boundaries of this consensus unspecified. Some sociologists such as Wallis (1976)
therefore argue for a more structural (organizational)

definition of cult. Wallis sees a cult as indeed theologically deviant but, more importantly, loosely organized, with transient members in a state of high turn
over, nonexclusive, and with little articulated authority structure. Says Wallis (1976:14), "The cult has no
clear locus of final authority beyond the individual
member." This accounts for the short life of so many
cultic groups. Cults are, in his words, "fragile institutions" with not only "doctrinal precariousness but also minimal organization." If simple theological deviance were the criterion for being a cult, asks Wallis,
how would we differentiate a cult from a sect (a sect,
according to sociologists, is a schismatic reform movement, made up of charismatic leaders and highly committed converted followers who have withdrawn from the
world but remain within a religious tradition, unlike a
cult) which also possesses deviant characteristics?[4]

A mixed model of cults combining both cultural and
organizational features and now accepted by most sociologists as definitive is that of Nelson (1969). Nelson
typified a cult as:

1.   Usually short-lived.

2.   Composed of individuals who have had or
      seek personal mystical, psychic, or ec-
      static experiences.

3.   A loosely structured movement having min-
      imal organization (usually a group of
      disciples or believers led by a charismatic
      teacher/guru).

4.   Concerned mainly with the problems of in-
      dividuals.

5.   Making a fundamental break with the re-
      ligious tradition of the larger society
      in which the cult arises.

This definition is less arbitrary and considerably more precise than past efforts to designate what a cult is and what real groups represent cults. Its precision eliminates much of the raw ethnocentrism one finds in the use of the word "cult" by evangelicals. However, there is a cost in achieving that precision. Nelson's definition may well describe the UFO cult of Bo and Peep which wandered nomadically about the United States in the mid-1970s (see Balch and Taylor, 1976) or the garbage-eating Body, but also excludes many groups that we want to consider. What are we to make, in terms of Nelson's criteria, of groups such as the Unification Church, or the Hare Krishna, or Scientology? The Unification Church of Sun Myung Moon, for example, resembles a cult in that it has a charismatic leader. One could claim (though not without argument) that it makes a significant break with dominant Christian religious traditions and that it attracts perons interested in improving or expanding what they are spiritually. However, the Unification Church is hardly a simple cult in many other respects. It has survived over a quarter of a century. (Where does one draw the line at "short-lived" in Nelson's definition?) It is actively seeking individual change only as part of a more explicit, doctrinally central goal of reshaping the economic/political/ educational/ scientific/religious institutions of the world, and is currently arguing for its place within the broader Christian tradition. Moon's movement in the United States alone owns newspapers, holds annual international conferences, runs a complete seminary, holds the deeds to millions of dollars worth of property and engages in a wide variety of industries, and is managed by a fairly sophisticated bureaucracy made up of accountants, legal experts, junior executives, and public

relations personnel. Its goals and its structure actually disqualify it as a cult on the first and third of
Nelson's characteristics and possibly also on Nelson's
second, fourth, and fifth characteristics. (We could
tell if he defined them more specifically.) Yet the Unification Church is one of the largest, best publicized,
and most representative (in terms of its deviant status)
of the "new religions" in twentieth century America and
certainly one of the first groups to be mentioned when
anti-cultists begin their shrill warnings about "cults".

Thus, specific definitions for terms such as "cult",
"sect", and so forth are useful for sociological analysis of various groups, but in light of our broader purposes they may exclude some organizations which have
been examined by scholars. Furthermore, the broad, rather
heterogeneous criteria by which scholars of various backgrounds classify groups as fringe or beyond the pale require us to maintain a more inclusive term. For this
reason I shall use the adjective "fringe" to refer to
all religions as defined earlier, i.e., as groups that
become the object of study by scholars trying to understand their departures from whatever existing norms of
belief and organizational practice these scholars perceive as customary in their societies.

ALTERNATE INTERPRETATIONS
OF FRINGE RELIGIOUS BEHAVIOR

There is a rich tradition in sociological thought,
in part an inheritance from its roots in philosophy, em-
phasizing the social origins of what we know and how we
know it. It is called the "sociology of knowledge" and
draws on the work of writers such as Max Weber, Karl
Marx, Alfred Schutz, and George H. Mead. The sociology

of knowledge's overarching premise is that people's understanding of social events and relationships is not only conditioned by their previous experiences and expectations but also influenced by the histories of their groups and values, and the threat or advantage to their personal interests posed by what they are viewing. Persons of similar backgrounds, in other words, will tend to rely on similar, predictable perspectives to give events and interactions meaning. THIS MEANING IS THE EMERGENT, ARRIVED-AT PRODUCT OF TACIT NEGOTIATION AND AGREEMENT BY THOSE SOCIAL ACTORS AND IS NOT INHERENT IN ACTION ITSELF. The act of taking another person's life, for instance, is not considered by a society anti-social or reprehensible per se. It depends upon who performs such an act and under what conditions (a policeman shooting a suspect during a bank robbery, a soldier bombing enemy cities during wartime, or a man stabbing his wife after a quarrel). The criteria which declare an act murder (or justifiable homicide or manslaughter or whatever label it is given) are socially decided upon, and courtroom trials dramatically illustrate how the legal institution meticuously assembles evidence to decide if an act was committed in the first place and then, if so, how to interpret it.

This process of establishing meaning is a social process which Berger and Luckmann (1967) term "the social construction of reality". Accordingly, the members of different groups will not always operate in terms of the same "social reality". That is, on those occasions when their assumptions greatly differ, they will not agree on what is "really happening" in a situation. Because so many persons tend to live their lives within the same culture and even subculture in which they were born and raised, they frequently are not challenged to question alternatives to their familiar social reality nor do they realize that persons of other cultures and subcultures premise their daily interactions on different sets of taken-for-granted assumptions about the way the world works. One broadly defined purpose of education, it might be said, is to provide just such an intellectual challenge. Anyone leaving an occidental culture and residing for a time in an oriental country, if he or she lives as a native of that country does and not surrounded by former countrypersons and lifestyle, quickly comes to appreciate the arbitrariness of the former social reality in such areas as ethics and courtesy.

Since most persons are accustomed to regard social facts as they do facts of the physical world, a brief example may better convey my point. Geologically speaking, a rock of basalt has a standard physical reality, from its appearance down to its molecular structure, that is not affected by the person who studies it, whether he is a Republican Protestant geologist in Kansas or an atheistic engineer in communist China. True, chemists and physicists might emphasize different properties of the rock, but those properties are nonrelative. The rock's hardness, color, weight, and other geological meanings remain completely independent of the particular scientist's religious values, political beliefs, and lifestyle preferences. This is obviously not the case with the social meanings of something like religion. Even when a pattern in social life has been certified as "objective" (i.e., various observers working independently confirm its existence) its social meaning still resides in the eye of the beholder. Take the case of church membership in many mainline Protestant denominations. According to regular surveys conducted by the National Council of Churches, in the late 1970s membership declines were found for the (northern)

United Presbyterian Church, the (southern) Presbyterian Church in the United States, the Episcopal Church, the United Church of Christ, the United Methodist Church, and both major Lutheran denominations, among others --though not for fundamentalist/evangelical/pentecostal groups. (See National Council of Churches, 1980.) No one disputes the factuality of the trends. Indeed, a number of these denominations at their recent annual conventions have spent much energy discussing possible causes and solutions for the membership drops. But what do these declines mean? Should we express satisfaction or gloom? Are they healthy signs, signalling America's turn from overbuilt, stale, unresponsive, middle-class denominations to creative, fulfilling, electric religious forms more compatible with a technologically sophisticated, cosmopolitan culture (demonstrating that the religious impulse never dies but constantly regenerates itself)? Or conversely, are they cause for foreboding, further evidence that permissive secularism and unbridled materialism are eroding the bedrock institutions of American morality, directly the church and indirectly the family and education (reaffirming that the liberalization of many churches and their involvement in social problems such as civil rights during the 1960s were colossal mistakes from which the mainline denominations may never recover)? Clearly an atheist might be expected to interpret this decline in terms of a different social reality than would a Methodist bishop. The patterns of membership decline are clear; their meaning, however, depends on one's expectations for American religion and the latter's future role in both public and private spheres. The patterns of decline are objective, their interpretation subjective.

The point of all this is that professional observers, like anyone else, bring to the study of fringe re-

ligions different perspectives to use in their analysis.
They operate out of only partially overlapping social
realities that are the intellectual products of separate
lines of professional training, disciplinary specializa-
tion of subject matter, and professional rewards. Most
of the time professionals in different disciplines do
not regularly interact. Often we only become aware of
their separate perspectives when they convene their attention on the same subject, as is the case here. However, the separation of knowledge into disciplines represents more than just a convenient division of labor.
Each discipline is, for all intents and purposes, something of an autonomous intellectual fiefdom that periodically engages in trade, correspondence, and diplomatic
exchanges with others but which nevertheless keeps to
itself a unique tradition of concepts and approaches to
understanding the world which it passes on to its students. As a result, while they may be studying the same
groups, they are not "seeing" the same groups.

   I believe this phenomenon of (often radically) different ways of constructing reality is well illustrated
by the scholarly literature on fringe religions. In
this book I have selected what I believe to be the six
major clusters of scholarly (as opposed to popular)
views regarding fringe religions. For each cluster I
have also chosen exemplary research works to be discussed. These clusters or perspectives are outlined in
Table I. Alongside each is a unique "unit of observation" (or dominant type of datum) by which it can be
identified.[5]

   In the "criminological" perspective fringe religious groups threaten the state's sovereignty by perform-
ing disloyal acts, or they may pose threats to the other

TABLE I

SCHOLARLY PERSPECTIVES IN
THE STUDY OF FRINGE RELIGIONS

Perspective	Unit of Observation
CRIMINOLOGICAL	
Subversive	Acts of a group's members which cause the state to define the group as disloyal
Exploitive	Acts of a group's leadership which deprive naive members of certain freedoms and resources guaranteed to be safeguarded by the state
PHILOSOPHICAL	Contents of beliefs and doctrine and their continutities/ contrasts with existing legitimate belief systems
ANTHROPOLOGICAL	Rituals, beliefs, and practices of religions as indices of social change
SOCIAL PSYCHOLOGICAL	Acts of group members thought to reveal certain psychological processes
SOCIAL STRUCTURAL	Recurrent patterns of interaction within groups as well as between groups and their social environment
HISTORICAL	Patterns of meaning constructed from the continuities between antecedent events and later events

citizens of a society by attempting to deprive them of specific freedoms and/or resources without these citizens' awareness that this is the goal of the group leadership. In the former (subversive) case the religious group's action is a direct challenge to the authority of the state, hence fundamentally illegal in almost any political jurisdiction. The goal may be a weakening of the state's authority or even its extinction. In the latter (exploitive) case, the victim is a member of the society. Exploitive criminal acts also constitute an indirect threat to the state, however, in view of sovereign laws which forbid overt exploitation of citizens in order to preserve internal order.

The philosophical perspective focuses on the idetional dimensions of fringe religions. The latters' doctrines and beliefs are scrutinized for internal consistency in order to judge if they are credible candidates for the next state of examination: comparative analysis using established religious traditions as standards of reference. This perspective also attempts to estimate the contribution or injury to existing systems of ideas which can be expected from the challenging doctrines of fringe religions.

The anthropological perspective views fringe religions as indices of social change. Like accusations of witchcraft, the emergence of fringe religions is considered by anthropologists to be a "strain gauge" in society. Such groups are believed to proliferate in times of rapid, stressful transition. The particular configuration of beliefs, rituals, and group organization is further thought to reflect these social strains. The widespread phenomenon of "cargo cults", which we will consider in detail, provides a prime example by which to examine the assumptions of the anthropological perspective.

The social psychological perspective is probably the most popular in western society. It fits comfortably with our traditional individualistic orientation and is a natural derivative of our daily experience. After all, everyone uses the actions of other persons to estimate their intentions and form impressions of their underlying personalities. Since even common sense tells us that attitudes and behaviors frequently coincide, the social psychological approach's assumption that mental states can be inferred from actions has been readily accepted both by the public and by many more serious observers of fringe religions.

The social structural perspective does not ignore cultural, psychological, or philosophical aspects of fringe religions. Indeed, social behavior would be unintelligible without knowing them. However, this sociological approach focuses on patterns of interaction, i.e., the organizational as opposed to the individual level. It views fringe religions as organizations subject to the same problems and needs as businesses or any other human activity involving groups of persons, asking questions about how they grow and survive. Admitting my bias beforehand, I find superior, on occasion, this interactionary approach in terms of avoiding the various pitfalls of personal bias and conceptual level-hopping found in other approaches and which will be illustrated in the following pages.

The final perspective, the historical, is concerned with constructing a context of meaning from discrete, isolated events that nevertheless have prior conditions out of which they develop and which help us understand them. While such a perspective might seem to offer the danger of every researcher reading into history his or her own personal biases and expectations, in actuality,

historians operate according to specific rules of evidence that mitigate against such unrestrained prejudice.

A final word before tackling each perspective in
subsequent sections: I have no wish to disparage other
disciplines or to imply that their approaches are inappropriate. Each offers only a partial view of fringe
religions, however, operating out of a distinct social
reality. Any negative comments or criticisms that follow, therefore, are not addressed to the validity of a
given approach per se but rather to tendencies of over-
stepping the limits of its assumptions in the practitioners' conclusions. With that caveat stated, let us
now see what "sense" different observers have been making
out of some extraordinary human activity.

NOTES

[1]David Bromley and I once wrote just such a caricature of a Catholic convent's lifestyle, entitled "The
Tnevnoc Cult" (convent spelled backwards), in order to
show that it is not the practices per se of a group that
earn it a reputation as strange or dangerous but rather
its social definition by power holders (i.e., "the establishment") in conventional society. By comparing the
treatment of Catholics (and the stories circulated about
them) in the United States during the early nineteenth
century with the treatment of the followers of "new religions" in modern American society--but not giving away
who the Tnevnoc's really were--we tried tongue-in-cheek
to put the current "cult" controversy into historical
perspective. Most professionals saw through the ruse.
However, a few contacted us seeking more information
about this mysterious "cult"! (See Bromley and Shupe,
1979).

[2]A good example of the anti-cult movement's tendency to draw increasing number of nonmainline groups under the "cult" umbrella can be seen in the following anecdote. In a _Playboy_ magazine interview (Siegelman and Conway, 1979: 220) Ted Patrick, the founder of deprogramming and arch-nemesis of all "cults", even included President Jimmy Carter's evangelist sister, Ruth Carter Stapleton, as "one of the biggest cult leaders in the nation." Patrick claimed that Stapleton employed "hypnotic techniques in her faith healing," sometimes on government officials. He said: "I saw one Cabinet Member on TV talking about how he was born again through Ruth Carter Stapleton. He looked just like a Moonie, glazed eyes, the works." Patrick did concede, however, that she was a "good cult leader," leaving open the possibilility that Dale Carnegie and a host of other hitherto unsuspected persons were in reality cult leaders, akin to the "white witches" of contemporary paganism.

[3]In fact, empirically speaking mainline theological consensus is a fiction, as Glock and Stark themselves (1965) and Hadden (1969) have shown in massive studies, respectively, of what lay parishioners and clergymen in various denominations actually believe. Glock and Stark found, for example, that Southern Baptists have more in common doctrinally with Roman Catholics than they do with Presbyterians. This should not seem unreasonable, given a little reflection. How many liberal Episcopalians would feel at home in the fundamentalist Biblical literalism of the Pentecostal Holy Tabernacle of the Pillar of Fire and Righteousness?

[4]Since I discuss cults only to illustrate the conceptual problems in attempting to refer to all nonmainline religious groups by a single term, I will not review in detail the larger literature on organizational

classification. Suffice it to say that the many arguments over the distinctions between church and sect, and
sect and cult, can easily lead one into confrontation
with an intellectual tar baby. I will address the
church-sect literature in "The Social Structural Perspective."

[5]It is important, I believe, to emphasize that by
unit of observation I do not mean the unit about which
conclusions are made but rather the true unit of analysis on which conclusions are based. Readers will find
it useful to bear this distinction in mind since in some
studies conclusions are drawn as to qualities of B when
only data on A have been collected. The conceptual
shift seems most frequently to occur from cultural to
psychological levels. Although these are analytical
levels, such conceptual shifts have real consequences in
research. We are clearly talking about something different when we speak of a given group's formal dogma or
beliefs as opposed to when we generalize about an individual's conception of those ideals, his motives for
joining the group, and so forth. Many researchers, however, out of a desire to "short-cut" analysis and bring
it in line with their value judgments or perhaps due to
the irresistible thrill of playing armchair Freud, will
take a cultural measure of a fringe religion, such as
its doctrine, and blithely draw psychological conclusions about members from it. To put the dangers of such
an improper scholarly practice in perspective, one could
be as seriously inaccurate in doing this with fringe religions as to assume liberal responses from a random
sample of southern white Americans in the early sixties
to racial minority protests solely on the basis of the
thoughts contained in the Constitution of the United
States.

REFERENCES

Berger, Peter and Thomas Luckmann. 1967. The Social Construction of Reality. Garden City, NY: Doubleday Anchor.

Balch, Robert and David Taylor. 1976. "Salvation in a UFO." Psychology Today 10 (October): 58-62, 66, 106.

Bromley, David G. and Anson D. Shupe, Jr. 1979. "The Tnevnoc Cult." Sociological Analysis 40 (Winter): 361-66.

Dohrman, H.T. 1958. California Cult: The Story of Mankind United. Boston: Beacon Press.

Glock, Charles Y. and Rodney Stark. 1965. Religion and Society in Tension. Chicago: Rand McNally.

Hadden, Jeffrey K. 1969. The Gathering Storm in the Churches. Garden City, NY: Doubleday Anchor.

Herberg, Will. 1960. Protestant, Catholic, Jew. (Revised edition) Garden City, NY: Double Anchor.

Kennedy, Ruby Jo Reeves. 1952. "Single or Triple Melting Pot? Intermarriage Trends in New Haven, 1870-1950." American Journal of Sociology 58: 589.

Lofland, John. 1966. Doomsday Cult. Englewood Cliffs, NJ: Prentice Hall.

Martin, Walter R. 1977. The Kingdom of the Cults. (Revised edition) Minneapolis: Bethany Fellowship.

Moos, Felix. 1964. "Some Aspects of Park Chang No Kyo: A Korean Revitalization Movement. Anthropological Quarterly (July): 110-20.

National Council of Church. 1980. Yearbook of American and Canadian Churches. Nashville: Abingdon Press.

Nelson, Geoffrey K. 1969. "The Spiritualist Movement and the Need for a Redefinition of Cult." Journal for the Scientific Study of Religion 8 (Spring): 152-60.

Schiffer, Wilhelm. 1955. "New Religions in Postwar Japan." Monumenta Nipponica 11 (April): 114.

Shupe, Jr., Anson D. and David G. Bromley. 1980. The New Vigilantes: Deprogrammers, Anti-Cultists and the New Religions. Beverly Hills, CA: Sage.

Siegelman, Jim and Flo Conway. 1979. "Playboy Interview: Ted Patrick." Playboy (March): 53ff.

Wallis, Roy. 1977. The Road to Total Freedom: A Sociological Analysis of Scientology. New York: Columbia University Press.

SUGGESTED FURTHER READING

Clark, Elmer T. 1965. The Small Sects in America. Nashville: Abingdon Press.

Durkheim, Emile. 1965. The Elementary Forms of the Religious Life. Trans. by J.W. Swain. New York: The Free Press.

Greeley, Andrew. 1972. The Denominational Society. Glencoe, IL: Scott, Foresman & Co.

Hoge, Dean R. and David A. Roozen, eds. 1979. Understanding Church Growth and Decline 1950-1978. New York: The Pilgrim Press.

Mann, W.E. 1955. Sect, Cult and Church in Alberta. Toronto: University of Toronto Press.

Mannheim, Karl. 1936. Ideology and Utopia. Trans. by Louis Wirth and Edward Shils. New York: Harcourt, Brace & World, Inc.

McFarland, H. Neill. 1967. The Rush Hour of the Gods. New York: MacMillan.

Mead, George H. 1962. *Mind, Self & Society*. Ed. by Charles W. Morris. Chicago: University of Chicago Press.

Moberg, David O. 1962. *The Church as a Social Institution*. Englewood Cliffs, NJ: Prentice-Hall, Inc.

Needleman, Jacob and George Bakers, eds. 1979. *Understanding the New Religions*. New York: Seabury Press.

Robbins, Thomas and Dick Anthony, eds. 1980. *In Gods We Trust: New Patterns of American Religious Pluralism*. New Brunswick, NJ: Transaction Press.

Schutz, Alfred. 1970. *On Phenomenology and Social Relations*. Ed. by Helmut R. Wagner. Chicago: University of Chicago Press.

Wach, Joachim. 1967. *Sociology of Religion*. Chicago: University of Chicago Press.

Weber, Max. 1964. *The Theory of Social and Economic Organization*. Trans. by A.M. Henderson and T. Parsons. New York: The Free Press.

Wilson, Bryan R. 1959. "An Analysis of Sect Development." *American Sociological Review* 24 (February): 315.

Yinger, J. Milton. 1946. *Religion in the Struggle for Power*. Durham, NC: Duke University Press.

_____. 1967. *Sociology Looks at Religion*. New York: MacMillan.

THOUGHTS FOR FURTHER CONSIDERATION

Anthropologists have developed the idea of "cultural relativism" (i.e., that various cultures should be studied as simply different and not have these differences judged as better or worse than others) as a methodological strategy. As a fieldwork tool it permits a scientist to suspend his personal value judgments and feelings about the truth or falsity of a foreign culture's beliefs and get on with describing and analyzing them. Developed into an ideology, cultural relativism negates the ultimate moral superiority of any belief or practice over any other. In the extreme cases, for example, cannibalism, rape or war atrocities have no inherent immorality other than what societies arbitrarily assign them. They simply exist. To what extent can we make absolutist statements about ethics and the morality of human relationships? Comparative social scientists claim the universality of certain basic norms (such as reciprocity and protection of in-group members, particularly family/guests) but exceptions can easily be found. Beyond various perspectives, is there a truth, or reality to be found?

THE CRIMINOLOGICAL PERSPECTIVE

It is not a far leap of imagination to move from
the observation that a fringe religious group is "odd"
to a sense that its religious challenge really poses a
serious potential threat to one's way of life and valued
social relations. Persons who adopt the criminological
perspective have made such a leap, sometimes on the basis of solid evidence (but also sometimes not). Their
obvious underlying assumption is that things are not as
they are claimed, that some crime or immoral act has
been perpetrated by a group "passing" as a bonafide religion. Since the inviolability of free religious belief is a sacred proposition drummed into the head of
anyone who ever sat through a high school civics class,
proponents of this perspective are usually quite vocal
about profoundly respecting religious freedom and pro-
fessing to be interested only in the activities of
fringe religions. When a group's beliefs are mentioned
at all by a writer in this perspective (assuming it is
not a lawyer monitoring the legal squabbles), it is usually to point up the discrepancies between ideals and
alleged deeds. In some cases these fringe beliefs
(which otherwise might involve considerable investment
of time and energy to assimilate) may be simply dismissed as incomprehensible jibberish or simply a cover for a
group's nefarious dirtywork.[1]

In this chapter I want to consider the two main variations of the criminological perspective. The first
variation deals with those actions of fringe religion

which serious observers have interpreted as subversive
to their society. Such subversion can be considered out-
right political and conspiratorial in the classic sense
or merely an eroding immoral influence on cherished institutions. The second variation of the criminological
perspective is concerned with the allegedly exploitive
actions of certain groups that are said to defraud, or
con, naive citizens out of their money, time, or even
personal liberty.

THE SUBVERSION THEME

Suspicion of the "new religions" and changing religious trends on the part of the "establishment" via
its "legitimate" observers seems to be as entrenched a
part of American religious traditions as the fact that
such groups are continually cropping up. Our present
era is not the first to hear alarms raised over the imminent danger to the Republic and its sacred institutions from "anti-social" religious sects and other challenging departures from orthodoxy. For example, the
well remembered seventeenth century colonial minister,
historian and defender of the infamous Salem "Witch Trials", Cotton Mather, believed that the eastern seaboard
North American colonies represented a new Israel preserved by God for the Puritans:

> The New Englanders are a People of God settled
> in those, which were once the Devil's Terri-
> tories; and it may easily be supposed that the
> Devil was exceedingly disturbed, when he per-
> ceived such a People here accomplishing the
> Promise of old made unto our Blessed Jesus,
> That He Should have the Utmost parts of the
> Earth for his Possession.

Yet, while Mather could bring himself to tolerate the quasi-mainline Presbyterians, Episcopalians, Congregationalists, and Anabaptists as "less but hopeful Attainments in Christianity," he had considerably more difficulty with unchurched more sectarian citizens who by the 1680s had turned much of the theocratic Puritan Massachusetts Bay Colony (including Salem) into a thriving cosmopolitan center of commerce. He was appalled by the profanity, sabbath breaking, drinking, and "whoring" of these new inhabitants as well as by the shocking diversity of religion he saw emerging. He was not alone among the old guard colonists who found it difficult to cope with the rapid socio-economic transition of the colony (Bednarski, 1970). Convinced that it was all a literal Satanic conspiracy, exemplified by a rise in witchcraft, Mather wrote of

> An Horrible Plot against the Country by Witchcraft, and a Foundation of Witchcraft . . . which if it were not seasonably discovered, would probably Blow up, and pull down all the Churches in the Country. And we have now with

Horror seen the Discovery of such a Witchcraft. Mather conceived of an "orgy of Devils" led by Lucifer who were aligned against God and the colony:

> Most horrible woes come to be inflicted upon Mankind, when the Devil does in great wrath make a descent upon them. (See, Mather, 1974: 11-43 for all quotes.)

(Such a model of human affairs and theory of fringe religions did not die with Mather; readers are referred to the subsequent chapter on the Philosophical Perspective for twentieth century examples.)

Most historians now attribute the supposed outbreak of witchcraft generally to the social strains experienced by the changing Massachusetts Bay Colony and

specifically to the religiously inspired adolescent neu-
roses of a few young girls who made the first accusations.   There was, in fact, no outbreak of witchcraft
but   rather   a   more   socially   explainable   outbreak   of
witchcraft persecution.   However, much of North America's legal tradition has involved real groups that, at
least in the minds of many, by their nonconforming actions were disloyal and posed a serious menace to social
order.   There are similar instances in American history
of conspiratorial hysteria.   The Irish Catholic immigrants during the mid-1800s experienced it.   Freemasons,
now one of modern America's most establishment oriented
civic clubs, as well as Mormons suffered hostility from
similar   reactionary   anti-movements (Davis, 1960).   The
Quakers fared no better at escaping persecution when it
was their turn.   More modern groups like the Jehovah's
Witnesses refusing to salute the American flag or to
serve in the armed forces, the Native American Church
seeking to preserve its right to use the peyote drug in
its religious services, Amish groups keeping their children out of public schools or resisting innoculation
from disease by public health officials, or the Mormons
practicing polygyny have had the labels of "disloyal" or
"subversive" applied to them, and as a result they have
had to argue for co-existence or even the right to existence in courtroom battles.   The legal reviews of these
cases   have   demonstrated   that   proving   subversion   by   a
group with some odd characteristics but yet perfectly
moral in other respects has not been easy for critics of
many fringe religions.   The complicated legal definition
of and eventually successful struggle to ban snake han-
dling among certain fundamentalist sects in the South
(see Flowers, 1979) and the eventually unsuccessful crusade of Christian missionaries to stamp out the use of
peyote in southwestern United States Indian religion

(see Lanternari, 1963: 63-100) are two such cases in which religious practices were accused of being harmful to participants in their respective groups and ultimately subversive to the health and values of larger society.

On the face of it, evaluating actions (and not beliefs) of fringe religions might seem uncomplicated. It is deceptively so, if history can teach us anything. However, Richard Delgado, a professor of law and outspoken critic of fringe religions as subversive during the 1970s and 1980s, pictures the process as a rather straight-forward task:

> A person may believe in a system which society labels bizarre or ridiculous but the state has no power whatsoever to interfere. It is when religious belief spills over into action that the degree of protection afforded to an individual or group is no longer absolute . . . .
> There **appear** to be no insuperable constitutional, moral, or public policy obstacles in the way of state or federal action designed to curb the abuses of of religious groups that utilize high pressure, harmful, and deceptive tactics in recruiting and indoctrinating young members. (Delgado, 1980: 25, 33)

(Dr. Delgado once advocated "consumer rights" legislation for persons being religiously missionized. The proposed legislation even included a mandatory "cooling off period" for new converts. Another idea which he advocated was the government licensing of religious recruiters. See, AFF, 1979)

Most legal experts agree with at least the first part of Delgado's statement. Even religions must surrender some sovereignty in their secular affairs. In

reviewing a Supreme Court's sustainment of the conviction of a Mormon who illegally continued to practice
polygyny, Pfeffer (1974: 15-16) commented:

> With the theology of a religious group the
> government may have no legal concern; but
> where its practices trench upon or threaten
> such important secular interests as the integ-
> rity of the monogamous family or of human
> life, it may and indeed must intervene for the
> protection of these interests.

Yet, as Pfeffer also acknowledged, despite the fact that
in the United States legal system there are formally no
"legitimate" or "marginal" religions, in reality these
distinctions are made in the informal assumptions of
judges and juries just as they are by tax officials who
must decide (on the basis of less arbitrary guidelines)
the legal status of groups applying for religious tax
exemption, literally passing judgment on a day to day
basis in the name of the state as to what is a "religion" and what is not for tax purposes. Fundamentally,
Pfeffer sees fringe religions as getting into trouble
not because of their beliefs per se but because of some
other activities of these groups. For example, how they
finance their operations, how their members live, or the
extent to which they cooperate with agencies such as
schools, public health offices, or the Internal Revenue
Service. Thus these fringe groups are perceived de-
stroying important institutions, presumably threatening
to violate broader social interests and (it is feared)
spreading if unchecked. This perceived direct threat to
social interests, for example, underlaid Christian missionaries attempts during the early part of this century
to outlaw the Native American Church's use of peyote in
its rituals. In one letter, read into the Congressional

Record (cited in Lanternari, 1963: 95), this charge was
bluntly put by an observer sympathetic to the Indians:
     It is the missionaries that are continually
     writing about the peyote orgies, etc. . . .
     Their fight is not based upon the actual phys-
     ical harm done to the Indians by the use of
     peyote--that is an excuse to offer the public
     --but it is because the Peyote Church is gain-
     ing more converts [among the Indians] than the
     missionaries . . . .
Social opinion becomes mollified and the tension
between group and society eases either when the group's
practices change[2] or when over the passage of time society itself changes and redefines the activity as non-
threatening. This was the case with the Jehovah's Witnesses. The many legal decisions in favor of the Wit-
nesses--who at one time were subjected to widespread mob
violence and intense public hostility--help gradually to
cool antagonism toward the group. From the standpoint
of the today's general public the sect has faded largely
into noncontroversial obscurity and is regarded as harm-
less (except by evangelical authors who continue to
write scathing condemnations which readers still can
easily purchase by the handful at their nearest Christian bookstore).
     What is the conclusion to be drawn from the legal
literature on subversion? It is that by and large
threat and subversion are matters of social agreement
and therefore are often subject to shifting mores and
prejudices. This legal reality (i.e., that popular con-
ceptions of what is mainline and what is fringe, however
temporary, influence lawmakers, judges, prosecutors, and
juries in deciding whether or not actions are subversive) has come to be a generally recognized fact of

American religious law.   For example, Burkholder (1974:
31) comments:

> Without denying the government prerogative to
> prohibit certain acts which may be deemed det-
> rimental to the larger public interest, we
> must recognize here the problem of majority
> versus minority opinion regarding the nature
> of "true religion". The sociology of knowl-
> edge helps us understand the prevailing opin-
> ion that the laws enacted by the majority are
> more representative of "true religion", than
> the claims made against them in the name of
> "true religion". In spite of protestations of
> neutrality with respect to belief, the process
> of adjudication has all too often been influ-
> enced by such presuppositions.

Pfeffer (1974: 20-24) cites, as a prime example of
popular values and assumptions slipping in to help interpret actions, the case of the I AM movement in which
its founder, an adventurer named Guy Ballard, claimed to
perform spiritual cures of real disorders and diseases
by mail for a fee. (A promotion which upset both postal
authorities and the American Medical Association.) The
judge admonished the jury not to try to decide the truth
or validity of the spiritual doctrine of Ballard's movement but rather to decide if Ballard and his assistants
themselves really believed the doctrine. (Needless to
say, Ballard provided plenty of defense witnesses who
really believed that they had been cured.) Ballard was
convicted of mail fraud. A more blatant instance of
popular prejudices influencing legal doctrines occurred
in the 1931 trial of Father Divine (alias George Baker)
as a public nuisance. Divine was a charismatic black
man who claimed to be God incarnate on earth. McKay

(1935: 153) like many, sensed conspiratorial elements in Divine's claim and in his interracial universalistic peace movement, stating, "Some cabalistic thing, such as exists in a secret society, may be at the bottom of this." Such suspicions were obviously part of Supreme Court Justice Lewis Smith's approach to the trial, since he violated practically all of Divine's civil rights during the proceedings, including cross-examining defense witnesses on their religious beliefs, issuing racist innuendos, mocking the defendant, openly criticizing Divine at the end in his charge to the jury, and even ignoring the jury's recommendation for leniency in its guilty decision. (Divine had the last laugh, however. The case was eventually overturned for obvious reasons. Moreover, the judge, otherwise healthy at 50 years of age, suddenly dropped dead of a heart attack four days after the trial. "I hated to do it," Divine reportedly commented. See, Harris, 1971: 31-44.)

The American anti-cult movement of the 1970s and 1980s naturally has offered grist for a number of scholarly mills. Most serious authors who have written of potential subversion in movements such as the Unification Church, Scientology, and the Hare Krishnas have also openly identified themselves as anti-cult partisans supporting preemptive repression of these groups (e.g., Boettcher and Freedman, 1980; Delgado, 1980; Levine, 1980; Conway and Siegelman, 1978; Cooper, 1971).[3] No doubt because of their professional training their writings typically display the usual scholarly restraints of providing evidence for assertions, qualifying generalizations, and refraining from the crude, ethnocentric hysteria found in more popular treatments such as Let Our Children Go! by deprogramming's founder, Ted Patrick (Patrick and Dulack, 1976). Moreover, those who see subversion in the current wave of new groups have given

an unintentional rise to their own antithesis by stimu-
lating a counter set of scholars and writings concerned
primarily with civil liberties (Kelley, 1977; Robbins,
1979). These latter authors, mostly lawyers, social
scientists, and liberal denominational representatives
or religious scholars, have in turn taken the proponents
of the subversion thesis to task by making much of the
rich historical pattern of "subversion finding" in America by comparing modern reactions to earlier ones.

THE EXPLOITATION THEME

To many serious observers (beyond cynical journal-
ists) the most important fact about fringe religions is
not their mere nonconformity or their theological "er-
rors" but rather that these groups presumably are con
games operated for profit under the constitutionally
protected cover of religion. Their leaders either are
considered deluded enough to believe their own bogus
claims of faith healing, spirit contact, messianic powers, and so forth or are suspected of willful deception
and fraud. In either case the net result is the same.
The gullible armies of seekers and believers, whether
little old ladies paying for seances or UFO messages or
college students dropping out of school and contributing
their stereo equipment to the guru, are naive victims.
Their gullibility and sincerity of interest in a given
group's bizarre but hopeful message only make their
perceived exploitation more tragic.

Actually whether the specific observer assumes that
a fringe leader is a conscious charlatan or is himself a
dupe of some larger scam can make some difference in the
fringe group's analytical treatment. For example, consider the following two scholarly evaluations of fringe
groups. The first is the conclusion of a supreme court
justice's statement in the trial of the I AM movement's
founder, Guy Ballard (United States v. Ballard, 1944--

cited in Pfeffer, 1974: 22):

> There are those who hunger and thirst after
> high values which they feel wanting in their
> humdrum lives. They live in mental confusion
> or moral anarchy and seek vaguely for truth
> and beauty and moral support. When they are
> deluded and disillusioned, cynicism and confu-
> sion follow. The wrong of these things, as I
> see it, is not in the money victims part with
> half so much as in the mental and spiritual
> poison they get. But that is precisely the
> thing the Constitution put beyond the reach of
> the prosecutor, for the price of freedom of
> religion or of speech or of the press is that
> we must put up with, and even pay for, a good
> deal of rubbish.

Rubbish is certainly not a very flattering euphemism for many fringe religions. The judge obviously
sees moral wrong and exploitation, but the larger cause
of civil liberties resigns him to more of a caveat emp-
tor philosophy. Contrast that evaluation with that of
Wilhelm Schiffer, a Jesuit priest writing about "New
Religions in Postwar Japan" during the mid1950s. After
a calm, thorough, scholarly treatment of these fringe
groups' doctrines and their continuities/discrepancies
with traditional religions, Schiffer (1955: 1314) unpre-
dictably launches into the following hostile condem-
nation:

> Their great number and the fervour of their
> believers certainly show that the interest in
> religious problems is by no means small. How-
> ever, when one sees the solutions given to
> these problems, one often cannot help feeling
> sorry for all those serious minded people who
> are being misled by religious quacks. For

this is the saddest part of the story of the
new religions in Japan: the spiritual unrest
of the people has been and is being abused by
unscrupulous crooks who see here an easy way
to fill their pockets quickly. . . . There
seem to be not a few who try to cover their
shady business operations with the pious cloak
of religion. The earnest longing for religious fulfillment, which is observed in a great
part of the population, especially also among
the younger generation, would deserve something better.

In general, observers who are not so concerned to
read wicked motives into the activities of fringe religious leaders and their groups engage more in a debunking operation than in practicing literary forensics.
It may be merely my own subjective impression, but they
also seem to do it with some wit, readability, and an
appreciation for the often sincere, earnest motives of
persons who would believe strange and outlandish beliefs.
Martin Gardner's Fads and Fallacies in the Name of
Science (1957) (which I will discuss as a case study later in this chapter) and Christopher Evan's classic
Cults of Unreason (1973) both in this genre, offer in-
formative tours de force of mystic messiahs from the
east, flying saucers cults, pyramidology, marginal
scientific and pseudo-scientific curiosities such as
dowsing, phrenology and palmistry, Orgonomy, Scientology
and even the Lock Ness Monster, all interlaced with good
humor that pokes fun but does not denegrate into malicious ridicule. L. Sprague De Camp's (1970) comprehensive
survey of the Atlantis-Lemuria lost continents theme in
literature and its dissemination throughout American occultism is another such study. At the conclusion of his

thorough, critical review of the foibles and religious inanities which have sought legitimation in the lost continent myths, De Camp can still retain a sense of the romantic spirit underlying his subject matter:

> Atlantis provides mystery and romance for those who don't find ordinary history exciting enough, and can be readily turned to account to point a moral lesson--in fact, any of many different and contradictory moral lessons. But most of all it strikes a responsive chord by its sense of the melancholy loss of a beautiful thing, a happy perfection once possessed by mankind. Thus it appeals to that hope that most of us carry around in our unconscious, a hope so often raised and as often disappointed, for assurance that somewhere, sometime, there can exist a land of peace and plenty, of beauty and justice, where we, poor creatures that we are, could be happy. (De Camp, 1970: 287)

In the same vein are Robert Wauchope's (1962) Lost Tribes and Sunken Continents, Owen Rachleff's (1971) The Occult Conceit, and parts of Colin Wilson's (1973) The Occult. Wauchope's book, for example, attempts to debunk religious theories of both lost continents and the origins of American Indians (that they are the "lost tribes" of ancient Israel and other "Jewish-Indian" theories that occupy a central place in the doctrines of sectarian groups such as the Mormons).

Compare these writings, generally empathetic as well as critical (as was De Camp in the previous quote), with some examples of authors perceiving criminal intent to defraud behind contemporary religious movements. Ignoring Ted Patrick's own unscholarly apologetic book,

Conway and Siegelman's (1978) Snapping claims that the
current wave of fringe religions has produced an epidemic of "information disease", i.e., alternating sen-
sory deprivation and overstimulation allegedly used by
"cults" in their recruitment, causing the mind to snap.
The book sees mind control of Unification Church members
by leaders as the explanation for their persistent fundraising activities in public places. After repeating
ex-members' horror stories of physical deterioration
from inadequate sleep and nourishment followed by reports of Moon's enormous personal wealth and his run-ins
with authorities, their clear implication is that Unification Church members are exploited by an ersatz messianic figure for gain (Conway and Siegelman, 1978: 2836).
They make similar cases against the International Society for Krishna Counsciousness (Hare Krishna), EST (Erhard Seminar Training), and Scientology. Likewise,
Stoner and Parke's All God's Children (1977), through
repeated leading rhetorical questioning and rather obvious innuendos, casts doubt on the religious inspiration
behind modern fringe religions. Other "cult" critiques
with a more theological orientation, such as Streiker
(1978) in his chapter entitled "Group Leaders, Greed,
and Coercion," and Enroth (1979) in a chapter entitled
"False Prophets and True Believers," devote some space
to suggesting openly that Rev. Sun Myung Moon, Guru
Marharaj Ji, and L. Ron Hubbard (the founder of Scientology) as well as Jim Jones have shared both megalomaniac aspirations and a desire for large amounts of
money.

I do not mean to imply either that Gardner et al.
ignore the substantial amount of fraud in American religion (they do not) or that Conway and Siegelman et al.
simply hallucinate improprieties where there are none

(they do not). My critical remarks of the latter group of authors should also not be taken to mean that I gloss over actual wrong doings. These authors obviously are responding to some very real events in society. In 1976, for example, several Scientologists did break into the office of an assistant U.S. Attorney in Washington, D.C. and riffle his files looking for documents relevant to their movement. In August, 1978 a Washington grand jury indicted eleven Scientologists on charges of burglary, bugging and obstruction of justice. In May, 1978 a Chicago-based sect, calling itself the Black Hebrews, was more than routinely watched by the FBI, not because of their religious beliefs but because there was good reason to believe the group had been assigning members to obtain jobs in banks as tellers and clerks in order to coordinate embezzlement schemes (with, allegedly, one million dollars to its credit already).

However, there is a tendency for the debunkers to approach each fringe group with initial suspicion but then to modify their views as each group respectively merits whereas such authors as Conway and Siegelman blanketly apply their judgments to a less clearly defined set of "cults". Moreover, the latter set of authors seems less able to discriminate between simply deviance and fraud. Fraud is a legal classification, with specific rules of evidence to decide it that are consensually arrived at by precedent and legal debate. Deviance is a social definition assigned by personal value judgments, and only when it seriously injures certain values important to social institutions (and can be shown empirically to injure them) can it be reclassified as crime. Certainly some religious leaders do live lifestyles that have all the comforts and privileges of millionaires. (Their defensive followers claim these

leaders own nothing themselves or only "use " the limou-
sines, yachts, and mansions owned by their incorporated
followers, but it is a distinction lost on nonmembers.)
Certainly those highly visible leaders such as Father
Divine or Rev. Moon have not used their millions of assembled dollars in ways that nonbelievers would define
as appropriate. And certainly families are torn apart
or terribly strained when one member enlists in a millenarian movement against the others' wishes. (The facts
that constitutionally guaranteed civil liberties protect
the right to join unpopular movements or that such family strains have a long tradition in the process of cultural renewal do not ease the personal anguish involved.) However, criminality is something considerably
more precise and calls for a much different response
from that to mere social deviancy. If adults freely wish
to exchange their lifestyles and resources for some in-
tangible spiritual commodity or condition, should we
oppose them, believing that we know better than they
what is in their best interest? If we do not use a
purely legal definition as a basis for deciding when
a group is criminal, then what will limit government
interference in fringe religious groups' activities?

These latter issues are currently the center of debate in the controversy over "new religions" and deprogramming. Deprogramming assumes that a young adult has
been manipulated through deception and psychological
techniques into losing his or her free will and then,
after this programming, is exploited to serve the whims
of sinister fringe religious leaders. To undo this process, a deprogramming is believed necessary. (The deprogramming is less systematic than its advocates would
like to admit. It consists mainly of physically abduct-
ing/restraining the person while the deprogrammer[s] and

family members force him to undergo a shocking confrontation with the anguish he has caused them and allegations of illegality about the fringe group.)

Much of the controversy really revolves around false issues, however. The accusation that all "cults" (as a gross stereotype) use manipulative, psychologically sophisticated and little known techniques to recruit and build conformity in members is vague, naive and empirically unsupported. The entire deprogramming rationale actually is a self-serving ideology adopted by the family to explain the younger member's rejection of its lifestyle and his defection to "the sounds of a different drummer." The deprogramming confrontation is a raw exercise of power by the family, which in many ways is more illegal than any dubious or misleading recruitment tactics purportedly used by any fringe religions (see Shupe and Bromley, 1980).

Father Divine and Daddy Grace, in their day, were credited just as Rev. Moon is now with enormous greed and mysterious powers of hypnosis, or mind control (see Harris, 1971), and many observers "assumed" criminal intentions in their activities. Where do deviance and crime begin? When does a believer's freely given sacrifice become a fringe leader's exploitation? The criminological perspective frequently gives us few guidelines to decide. Consider a final example which illustrates how bizarre actions (bizarre, that is, according to the standards of middle class white Christianity) can shift over the fine line into the gray area of apparent fraud. It is a brief excerpt from Fauset's (1970: 28) description of a religious service held in the United House of Prayer for All People, a largely black urban cult run by Bishop Charles Emmanuel "Daddy Grace" who was a contemporary, and competitor, of Father Divine in Harlem during the Depression.[4]

The bass drummer beats his drum and begins to
sing, aided by tambourines struck by women in
various parts of the room--one woman dressed
in red and making grimaces and queer gesticu-
lations beats very weird rhythms. Other men
and women clap their hands, while still others
clap two pieces of wood together. There are
cries of "Daddy! You feel so good!" "Sweet
Daddy!" "Come to Daddy!" "Oh, Daddy!". . .
More singing and dancing follows. Women become convulsed, contort themselves, cavort
through the house of prayer, finally falling
in a heap on the sawdust. They lie out-
stretched, inert. . . . The minister continues. He extols Daddy Grace soap, which he
claims will reduce weight. It has healing
properties also, he states. . . . The minister takes a copy of the Grace Magazine, which
sells for ten cents, and offers it for sale.
"Put this magazine," he cries, "on your chest
if you have a cold or the tuberculosis, and
you will be cured."

People have a constitutional right to work themselves into orgasmic trances, "cavort", and believe in
the supernatural status of one of their fellows. But
money accepted for the medical claims of the minister
could likely be another matter in court. (Guy Ballard
went to prison for making such claims.) It is precisely
such legal distinctions that need to be made in adopting
a criminological perspective. All nonmainline groups
are not crooked or "rip-offs". If there is an overall
weakness in this criminological approach, it is a cynical tendency to overgeneralize, to impute criminal intent to the actions of persons who believe radically

different doctrines from the popular norm and who organize their affairs in terms of different ideals than
those observers hold. In a word, its weakness is a frequent, arbitrary presumption of criminality in social
and cultural deviance which may not be warranted at all.

CASE STUDIES

The two case studies presented below illustrate the
two themes found within the criminological perspective.
Gifts of Deceit is an excellent example of the subversion type dealing with foreign conspiracy and scandal in
the Koreagate investigation—though it also contains accusations relevant to the exploitative type. Its solid-
ly researched exposure of the Korea government's attempts to buy influence in Washington gives a good contrast to its accompanying leaps of faith made in its
pronouncements about the Unification Church's involvement and motives. Martin Gardner's Fads and Fallacies
in the Name of Science represents one of the earlier examples of the debunking genre and lacks the grim sense
of purpose with which the authors of Gifts of Deceit
pursue their task.

FIRST CASE

Gifts of Deceit
Robert Boettcher (with Gerald L. Freedman)

"Koreagate" was the euphemism of the media for a
series of shocking revelations in the mid-1970s that the
South Korean government, under direct orders from the
highest places in the Park Chung Hee dictatorship, had,

since the beginning of the decade, been paying bribes to a number of U.S. officials in order to maintain high levels of U.S. military aid flowing into that Asian country. Gifts of Deceit is ostensibly a chronicle of how that scandal unfolded, from the progressive involvement of major figures like the Washington socialite-opportunist Tongsun Park to the formal investigations and hearings by the FBI and the House of Representatives. However, it is also an attempt to document Sun Myung Moon's Unification Church as a co-conspirator in Koreagate and to portray Moon as both a tool of the South Korean government and a money-hungry, arrogant pseudo-prophet.

Boettcher was the staff director of the House Subcommittee on International Relations, chaired by Representative Donald E. Fraser, and participated directly in supervising the several year investigation by the "Fraser committee" begun in 1976. (Freedman also was closely involved in the investigation.) In some ways Gifts of Deceit is simply a Boettcher-Freedman rehash (albeit a more readable one) of the lengthier, more ponderous U.S. Government publication entitled "Investigation of Korean-American Relations." In other ways, however, it goes beyond the subcommittee's report since it has more literary freedom to weave suspicions about Moon and his movement out of circumstantial evidence and hearsay than did the subcommittee's original report. Boettcher-Freedman, for example, describe top-secret meetings and innermost thoughts of persons attending these as if they (Boettcher-Freedman) were there, using the many interviews collected during the hearings as a guide. For some thoroughly investigated events in this country this style is convincing; for others taking place thousands of miles away in the back rooms of the

President's mansion in Seoul and depending on psychological second guessing it stretches a little thin.

At any rate, the incriminating evidence on the illegal activities of various South Korean embassy officials, Korean CIA agents, and U.S. Congressmen was me-
ticulously collected, and the Boettcher-Freedman version
of it reads like good Sherlock Holmes. Koreagate was a
very complex web of interlocking relationships involving
persons with various degrees of criminal intent and cul-
pability. Boettcher-Freedman visualize three key figures in Koreagate--President Park Chung Hee, Tongsun
Park, and Rev. Sun Myung Moon--and it is with the material on the third of these that this analytic survey of
studies of fringe religions is concerned.

According to Boettcher-Freedman the South Korean
government tried to use Sun Myung Moon and his neo-
Christian Unification Church about as much as the latter
tried to use Park's regime. It was portrayed as a sym-
biotic relationship in which the South Korean government
gave Moon unique preferential treatment under Park's
corrupt, repressive rule (permitting Moon to hold large
public rallies, awarding him lucrative government con-
tracts, and generally abstaining from harassing Moon's
movement in the same way that other Christian groups in
that country experienced) in exchange for both Moon's
militant anti-communist and theological support of the
Park regime and the Unification Church's efforts in the
United States to lobby for continued military support,
other aid, and good will for South Korea. Though the
authors state that Moon was the intended target of the
South Korean government's manipulation (Park certainly
did not subscribe to Moon's messianic doctrines or goals
for a world theocracy), they also point to his own conspiratorial ambitions that equally manipulated South

Korea and Park. Moon is portrayed as a shrewd, arrogant, hustling megalomaniac who only agreed to this
"deal" with Park as a matter of convenience:

> President Park and his influence planners may
> have thought they were using Moon for Korea.
> What they may not have realized was how much
> Moon was using Korea for himself. . . . He
> treats all governments, just as he treats all
> people, with contempt. People are mere step-
> ping stones to the throne he claims God has
> promised him. The path he treaded to power
> must be paved with important people. (338)

Through his translator and right-hand man, Bo Hi Pak,
the books claims that the right balance between Park's
interests and Moon's ambitions was struck, at least until Koreagate.

The emerging picture of the Unification Church,
based on both large amounts of government-subpoenaed interviews and documents and the authors' editorializing
is not only unflattering, it is downright sinister. The
Unification Church, we learn, is a "menance" that has
"invaded" the United States. Moon is an avaricious dem-
agogue obsessed with power, recruiting his naive followers by guile and deceit and exploiting them as literal
slaves. (Slaves and zombies are two analogues that keep
appearing whenever the movement's members are mentioned.) He is a charlatan, hiding behind the First Amendment:

> The American system is ill-equipped to deal
> with Moon. He knows this and benefits from
> it. He can break some laws and use others for
> protection. By perverting freedom of relig-
> ion, he can keep thousands of people in brain-
> washed captivity while he intimidates and man-
> ipulates the non-Moon world. (347)

Worst of all, the authors compare the Unification Church with the People's Temple and suggest that a Korean-style Jonestown is not unimaginable.

It is an indisputable fact that certain members of the Unification Church were involved in Koreagate. Given the Korean government's presumption that it could rough up and intimidate at will Korean residents in the United States (as the investigation clearly showed it did), it would be surprising if the Park regime had not approached Moon and his Korean elites for support. Considering also the fragile condition of religious freedom in South Korea since before the Japanese occupation (and Moon's personal experiences as a captive in communist labor camps), it is also no surpise that Moon would seek rapport with the militantly anti-communist government in Seoul.[5]

However, admitting that connection, the Boettcher-Freedman outline of the larger Moon movement is more of a caricature, founded in a number of poorly supported rumors and stereotypes, than an accurate portrait. Much of its information on the inner workings of the Church--fundraising, recruitment, lifestyle, and so forth--comes from disgruntled ex-members such as Allan Tate Wood, Christopher Edwards, and Chris Elkins who have gone on to write books about their experiences and join the speaker circuits as professional apostates. It draws on the testimonies of professional deprogrammers and angry parents of church members as proof of its allegations that the latter young people are half-starved, barely conscious automatons (both groups benefiting from such imagery). To give just two examples of the authors' extrapolation from hearsay: they claim a success rate for deprogramming of 95 per cent, and that wrist slashing, if captured by deprogrammers, is standard indoctrination fare for Moonies (two "atrocity stories" debunked in Shupe and Bromley, 1980).

Because of the muck already dredged up in the larger investigation, Boettcher-Freedman apparently went on to suspect the worst about the entire Unification Church. As they noted, the actual prosecution of Congressman or Koreans involved was meager, and when the smoke cleared, the only principal actors in the drama still remaining were the Moonies. This may have caused some frustration for the authors. For generating such suspicion the Church, of course, has to take partial blame. But Boettcher-Freedman's character assassination of Moon, based solely on a few of Moon's more grandiose, hyperbolic "insider" revival-style speeches (Moon himself never appeared before the Fraser committee) is unwarranted. Unwarranted also is their crude stereotyping of all Church members as mentally enslaved robots based only on testimony from the movement's avowed enemies when, by the late 1970s, a number of studies questioning this image were available. (See "The Social Psychological Perspective".) For these reasons Gifts of Deceit aptly demonstrates a number of dangers inherent in indiscriminate or unlimited application of the criminological perspective.

SECOND CASE

Fads and Fallacies in the Name of Science
Martin Gardner

At the outset it may seem inappropriate to readers for me to select a book such as Gardner's, or any other that I have previously categorized as a "debunker", since religious ideas cannot be "debunked". They are

not empirical truth claims but matters of faith and
therefore do not lend themselves to proof or disproof.

However, many of the targets of Gardner's analysis
are in a special class of fringe religions. These are
groups that employ some element of science or pseudo-
science in their doctrines or practices and that in fact
claim some scientific support for their spiritual validity. It is the scientific claims of such groups that
Gardner directly scrutinizes, though their religious
credibility also comes under attack at least implicitly.
The champions of Atlantis and Lemuria, for example,
whose occult lodges can be found across the United
States from the American Theosophical Society's head-
quarters in Wheaton, Illinois to the Order of the Ancient Mayans in San Antonio to the Rosicrucians (AMORC)
in San Jose, infuse their religious beliefs with geological, astronomical, and numerological "proofs". Scientology (once Dianetics) mixes its version of depth psychology with notions of reincarnation and a primeval
thetan-spirit which all persons originally possessed.
Likewise, there are still fundamentalist Christians in
the sciences trying to reconcile the findings of modern
evolutionist biology and geology with the Genesis account of creation or Mormons seeking archeological support for Jewish migration to North America before
Christ. These are not the only targets of Gardner's
critiques, as they are not the only ones of Evans and
Decamp mentioned earlier, but they appear enough in his
writings to justify their consideration in this survey
of fringe religious studies.

Gardner is a popular science writer and editor with
a strong penchant for ferreting out cranks and others
who believe in what the conventional wisdom says to be
hare-brained and preposterous. In fairness to Gardner,

he tends to take more seriously what others might simply
write off as crooked money-making schemes though he is
merciless in exposing their faulty premises. Because of
his fluid writing style, wry sense of humor, and erudi-
tion, it is tempting for the reader to accept Gardner's
critical descriptions of various groups and take comfort
in the feeling that mainline religion and mainline
science, whatever their limitations, still seem the best
(separated) options for truth after all. Rather than
attack a given group, fad, or cult with vicious serious-
ness, Gardner's technique for devastatingly discrediting
it is to make the target look silly. He does not play
on the reader's senses of outrage or paranoia but rather
on his sense of humor. (It is worth noting that no serious critic of contemporary fringe religions, to my knowledge, has employed humor as a weapon to oppose them.
Other than a short parody of the Unification Church
which I had shown to me in an issue of Mad Magazine,
sporadic references to Moonies in the cartoon strip
Doonesbury, and occasional political cartoons, the anti-
cult movement has chosen the mirthless rather than the
satirical route.) Gardner also counts on his readers
sharing his own middle-class assumptions about social
reality, i.e., that they will trust M.D.'s over osteo-
paths or chiropractors, that they understand the story
of Adam and Eve as an allegory rather than as literal
history, that they feel ESP is bunk and/or the result of
scientists and subjects deceiving themselves, and so
forth.

Gardner is not the first of the debunkers, as he
points out in his preface, but his literate, well informed style no doubt set the standard for later writers. For example, his essay on Dianetics, L. Ron
Hubbard's neo-psychoanalytic cult of the 1950s, is still

a masterpiece of logical dissection that was only lengthened but not improved by Evans (1973) and Cooper (1971). (Gardner wrote before Hubbard sought constitutional protection for his group in the United States as a religion and consolidated his movement into a more cohesive organization, but the premises of Hubbard's later form were already in Dianetics. See also Wallis' monograph on the subject discussed in "The Social Structure Perspective.") If there is a single criticism to be made of Gardner (and writers in the genre to which he contributed) it is that he accepts too comfortably the conventional wisdom, or accepted social reality, of current twentieth century science and middle-class American Christianity. Somehow it is evident (to me at least) that he is implicitly making a pact with the reader to evaluate these fringe groups in terms of their own shared presumptions about what is "normal". Thus he is quite confident throwing around labels like "quack", "crank", and "preposterous". In science the use of such value judgments can be quite time-bound; likewise in religion where today's heresy may become tomorrow's orthodoxy. The odds of course are always on the side of the writer criticizing fringe groups because statistically speaking so few of them survive. However, when a group does weather its infancy and go on to prosper, invariably its original detractors look a bit more arbitrary and even amusing than they did initially, and then the shoe is on the other foot.

NOTES

[1]In Ted Patrick's apologetic account of deprogramming and his personal crusade against the "cult menace" (Patrick and Dulack, 1976: 19) there is a conversation

between Joe Franklin (one of Patrick's assistants) and a
reporter on the topic of Sun Myung Moon's Divine Principle (the Unification Church's original scripture) that
illustrates this "know-nothing" approach to fringe doctrine:

> In the dining room, the reporter muses over a
> black book, resembling a Bible, entitled Di-
> vine Principle. It is incomprehensible. . . .
> "Course nobody can understand the damn thing,"
> Joe Franklin drawls. "That's the whole idea.
> Bernie's [the deprogrammee] never read it.
> They give them a study guide. It's all just a
> pile of junk."

[2]During the late 1970s the Unification Church,
aware of the enormous public uproar over its high pressure recruitment tactics, began to seek a new image
through "home missions". Individual members moved out
of communal church centers in some areas and rented
apartments in urban neighborhoods where they practiced
more Fabian tactics of general good neighborliness and
selective, gradual proselytization. This is an overall
strategy which has been used for years, apparently with
considerable success, by the Mormons. (See Stark and
Bainbridge, 1980.)

[3]There exists, of course, a veritable sea of pamphlets, paperback books, cassette recordings and films,
magazine articles, and more transitory sources such as
newsletters produced by the various organizations in the
anti-cult movement, all claiming that such-and-such
group is a subversive menace to the family, Judeo-
Christian religion, education, and the government. (See
Shupe, Bromley and Oliver, 1981; Shupe and Bromley,
1980.) Though nonscholarly in approach and style (and
therefore not directly considered here) these works have

many fascinating parallels with similar bodies of literature condemning other fringe religions throughout American history.

[4]Not to be outdone by Father Divine's claim that he
was God incarnate, Daddy Grace had his own self-apprais-
al which was equally outrageous to his critics. Grace
claimed he had given God a vacation and that "all you
need is Grace." (Pun intended. See Fauset, 1970.)

[5]The outrage of Boettcher-Freedman that the Unification Church as a legally recognized religious body
would dare lobby in Washington seems naive to anyone
familiar with church and state relations in the United
States. For years the National Council of Churches (among
others) has maintained a full-time office in Washington,
D.C., under the title of the Commission on Religious Liberty, precisely for the purpose of lobbying. (See
Morgan, 1968: 48-60.) Likewise, the Baptist Joint Committee on Public Affairs, an arm of the Southern Baptist
Convention, in 1979 maintained a ten-person staff with a
budget of $308,000. In a newspaper interview its head
official admitted to a reporter, "We're involved in lobbying, although we don't like to call it that." (As
Boettcher-Freedman pointed out, neither did the
Moonies.) The Baptists prefer the term "stewardship of
interest". (See "Where Church and State meet: Baptist
Group Trying to Show Congress the Light." Fort Worth
Star-Telegram, 9/23/79.)

REFERENCES

AFF. 1979. Transcript of Proceedings, Information Meeting the Cult Phenomenon in the United States.
Lexington, MA: American Family Foundation.

Beebe, Robert L. 1979. "Tax Problems Posed by Pseudo-
    Religious Movements." The Annals of the American
    Academy of Political and Social Science (Special
    Issue: The Uneasy Boundary: Church and State)
    November: 32-51.

Bednarski, Joyce. 1970. "The Salem Witch-Scare Viewed
    Sociologically." Pp. 151-63 in Max Marwick, ed.,
    Witchcraft and Sorcery. Baltimore, MD: Penguin
    Books.

Boettcher, Robert and Gordon L. Freedman. 1980. Gifts
    of Deceit: Sun Myung Moon, Tongsun Park, and the
    Korean Scandal. New York: Holt, Rinehart and
    Winston.

Burkholder, John Richard. 1974. "The Law Knows No Her-
    esy: Marginal Religious Movements and the Courts."
    Pp. 27-50 in Irving I. Zaretsky and Mark P. Leone,
    eds., Religious Movements in Contemporary America.
    Princeton, NJ: Princeton University Press.

Conway, Flo and Jim Siegelman. 1978. Snapping. New
    York: J.B. Lippincott.

Cooper, Paulette. 1971. The Scandal of Scientology.
    New York: Tower.

Davis, David Brion. 1960. "Some Themes of Counter-
    Subversion: An Analysis of Anti-Masonic, Anti-
    Catholic, and Anti-Mormon Literature." The
    Mississippi Valley Historical Review 47
    (September): 205-24.

De Camp, L. Sprague. 1970. Lost Continents: The
    Atlantis Theme. New York: Ballantine Books.

Delgado, Richard. 1980. "Limits to Proselytizing."
    Society 17 (March/April): 25-33.

_____. 1977. "Religious Totalism: Gentle
    and Ungentle Persuasion Under the First Amendment."
    Southern California Law Review 51 (November): 1-98.

Enroth, Ronald. 1979. The Lure of the Cults. Chappaqua, NY: Christian Herald Books.

Evans, Christopher. 1973. Cults of Unreason. New York: Dell.

Fauset, Arthur H. 1970. Black Gods of the Metropolis. New York: Octagon Books.

Flowers, Ronald B. 1979. "Freedom of Religion Versus Civil Authority in Matters of Health." The Annals of the American Academy of Political and Social Science (Special Issue: The Uneasy Boundary: Church and State) November: 149-61.

Gardner, Martin. 1957. (Revised Edition) Fads and Fallacies in the Name of Science. New York: Dover Publications, Inc.

Harris, Sara. 1971. Father Divine. (Revised Edition) New York: Collier Books.

Johansen, Robin B. and Sanford Jay Rosen. 1979. "State and Local Regulation of Religious Solicitation of Funds: A Constitutional Perspective." The Annals of the American Academy of Political and Social Science (Special Issue: The Uneasy Boundary: Church and State) November: 116-35.

Kelley, Dean M. 1977. "Deprogramming and Religious Liberty." The Civil Liberties Review 4 (July/August): 23-33.

Mather, Cotton. 1974. Cotton Mather on Witchcraft: The Wonders of the Invisible World. (Third reissue of the original 1692 edition) New York: Bell Publishing.

McKay, Claude. 1935. "'There Goes God!': The Story of Father Divine and His Angels." The Nation February 6: 15153.

Morgan, Richard E. 1968. The Politics of Religious Conflict. New York: Pegasus.

Patrick, Ted and Tom Dulack. 1976. Let Our Children
    Go! New York: Ballantine Books.
Pfeffer, Leo. 1974. "The Legitimation of Marginal Re-
    ligions in the United States." Pp. 9-26 in Irving
    I. Zaretsky and Mark P. Leone, eds., Religious
    Movements in Contemporary America. Princeton, NJ:
    Princeton University Press.
Rachleff, Owen S. 1971. The Occult Conceit. New York:
    Bell Publishing Co.
Robbins, Thomas. 1979. Civil Liberties, "Brainwashing"
    and "Cults": A Select Bibliography. Berkeley, CA:
    Program for the Study of New Religious Movements in
    America.
Schiffer, Wilhelm. 1955. "New Religions in Postwar
    Japan." Monumenta Nipponica 11 (April): 1-14.
Shupe, Jr., Anson D. and David G. Bromley. 1980.
    "Witches, Moonies, and Accusations of Evil." in
    Thomas Robbins and Dick Anthony, eds., In Gods We
    Trust: New Patterns of American Religious Plural-
    ism. New Brunswick, NY: Transaction Press.
Stark, Rodney and William Sims Bainbridge. 1980. "Net-
    works of Faith: Interpersonal Bonds and Recruitment
    to Cults and Sects." American Journal of Sociology
    85 (May): 1376-95.
Stoner, Carroll and Jo Anne Parke. 1977. All God's
    Children. Radnor, PA: Chilton.
Streiker, Lowell D. 1978. The Cults are Coming!
    Nashville: Abingdon Press.
Wauchope, Robert. 1962. Lost Tribes and Sunken Contin-
    ents. Chicago: University of Chicago Press.
Whelan, Charles M. 1979. "Governmental Attempts to De-
    fine Church and Religion." The Annals of the Amer-
    ican Academy of Political and Social Science (Spe-
    cial Issue: The Uneasy Boundary: Church and State)
    November: 32-51.

Wilson, Colin. 1973. The Occult. New York: Vintage
    Books.

SUGGESTED FURTHER READING

Cantril, Hadley. 1969. "The Kingdom of Father Divine."
    Pp. 223-42 in Barry McLaughlin, ed., Studies in
    Social Movements. New York: The Free Press.
Eliade, Mircea. 1976. Occultism, Witchcraft, and Cul-
    tural Fashions. Chicago: University of Chicago
    Press.
Krinsky, Fred. 1968. The Politics of Religion in Amer-
    ica. Beverly Hills, CA: The Glencoe Press.
Robertson, D.B. 1968. Should Churches Be Taxed?
    Philadelphia: The Westminister Press.
Shupe, Jr., Anson D., Roger Spielmann, and Sam Stigall.
    1977. "Deprogramming: The New Exorcism." American
    Behavioral Scientist 20 (July/August): 941-56.
Stark, Werner. 1967. The Sociology of Religion. Vol.
    2 "Sectarian Religion." New York: Fordham Univer-
    sity Press.
Starkey, Marion L. 1969. The Devil in Massachusetts.
    Garden City, NY: Doubleday Anchor.
Wilson, John. 1978. Religion in American Society: The
    Effective Presence. Englewood Cliffs, NJ:
    Prentice-Hall.

THOUGHTS FOR FURTHER CONSIDERATION

Legally, persons may believe anything they please in American society, but their actions frequently involve other people, and these actions are within society's domain to supervise. From a practical point of view, does a society (through its police, government agents, etc.) have a right to take preemptive, i.e., preventive, actions against a fringe religion which might pose a danger to citizens? Need we wait for a tragedy such as occurred at Jonestown, Guyana where over 900 persons, including children and the elderly, drank cyanide-laced Kool-aid and died, or can/should we act to intervene in groups we suspect of having such anti-social capabilities? If not, is Jonestown also a price our society paid for religious freedom? If so, who will decide when a group has anti-social capabilities?

THE PHILOSOPHICAL PERSPECTIVE

What I term the philosophical perspective or approach is used most often by historians and philosophers of religion, theologians, and other scholars in the broad area of religious studies. Its primary emphasis is on the doctrines of fringe religions, guided in its research by two important sets of questions.

The first set of questions asks for descriptive, internal information. What are the main beliefs of a given group and their origins? Are they internally consistent and systematic? What is the fit between those seminal doctrines identified and other important aspects of the the group? (What, for example, is the essence of the goal of an artistic life in PL Kyodan, a postwar Japanese new religion, and how does it relate to the group's conspicuous emphasis on playing golf?)

The second set of questions focuses on larger, external matters. No religious group, not even the most radical movement or cult, begins totally from scratch. It innovates, synthesizes, revitalizes familiar ideas --it does not create them anew. What are its continuities in older traditions and with contemporary ideas afloat in society at the time of its founding? What do its doctrines say differently from other groups? (For example, what elements of Korean folk shamanism, Confucian ethics, and imported fundamentalist Christianity did Sun Myung Moon draw upon before and after his teenage "revelation from God?)

It would be difficult for any scholar approaching even a single fringe religion not to ask simultaneously both types of questions. In studying the postwar Japanese new religions, for example, both McFarland (1967) and Offner and Van Straeland (1963) discuss a number of groups in terms of their continuities with older faith traditions, their overlapping doctrinal emphases, and their relations to the social changes of that region and postwar era. This is done on a group-by-group basis as well as according to certain key dimensions--charismatic leadership, ultimate goals, concept of deity, and so forth. While McFarland's study is more anthropological and Offner and Van Straeland are more interested in the healing beliefs and practices of such groups, there are nevertheless certain basic data needed to make sense out of any group's doctrines that these, and any other serious scholar utilizing the philosophical approach, would have to consider. This domain of core topics and dimensions becomes more complicated, of course, if fringe religious groups in one culture are transplanted to a radically new culture (where they look even more bizarre). Ellwood (1974) shows this in his study of those same Japanese new religions analyzed by McFarland and Offner and Van Straeland when they have been exported to the United States.

A distinct cleavage of opinions and basic assumptions about fringe religions into separate camps can be seen in analyses using a philosophical perspective. One camp, largely composed of evangelical Christians, takes a very dour view of such innovative groups and addresses their doctrines mainly for the purpose of refuting them. There is little rejoicing over religious pluralism here. These authors are also those most likely to employ the label "cult" indiscriminately (from a sociologist's standpoint) in referring to sectarian Christian and non-Christian groups alike. The other camp, mostly made up of non-evangelicals and liberal scholars, is more open to the possible contributions, on both cultural and individual levels, that such heretical or pagan fringe groups might make, and as a consequence it spends considerably less energy lambasting them. Fringe groups are not, at the outset, determined to be hopelessly in error.

THE EVANGELICAL RESPONSE

Those scholars unenthused about the emergence of fringe religions regard them, in the words of Van Baalen (1938: 14) over forty years ago, as "the unpaid bills of the church." The spiritual thirst of their members presumably reflects failure on the part of orthodox Christianity to get out its consummate message as completely as it ought to have. As a result, millions of persons have turned to heretical distortions of the true faith. In this vein Starkes (1972: 9) states:

> The fact is clear that the emergence of the
> Christian deviations is at least partially
> due to the neglect among evangelical Christians
> of "the edifying of the body of Christ" men-
> tioned in Ephesians 4:12 and I Timothy 1:4.
> This may best be termed as the sin of neglect.

Likewise, Davies (1972) terms the proliferation of Christian "deviations" (his term) as a scandalous "tearing of the seamless robe of Christ" (5) and a "betrayal of Christ's will for unity among his disciples." (1)

Evangelical criticism is not aroused by the sheer fact of religious pluralism per se (though it is tempting for an observer to conclude that religious pluralism per se is threatening to any form of fundamentalism).[1] Rather, these critics perceive fringe religious groups as definite threats to the doctrinal tradition of Jesus

Christ and magnets to draw sincere but naive persons
away from the true Christian faith. Says Davies (1972:
1): "Their very success in perpetuating error, strife,
and bitterness constitutes their challenge and menace
to the historic Christian churches." He continues (3):

> If their work were only among the pagans or
> the uncommitted of the modern world, then con-
> cern for their success might rightly be inter-
> preted as a dog-in-the-manger attitude. <u>The
> great danger, however, comes from the arrogant
> dogmatism with which most of them claim that
> they alone have the full and untainted truth
> and from their often successful attempts to
> steal sheep from other folds of the Christian
> Church.</u> (Emphasis mine.)

Indeed, as Coser (1956:70-7) notes in his review
of the early German sociologist George Simmel's writings
on group conflict, the heretic is a particularly insidious character from the standpoint of defenders of an
orthodox faith. Tibetan Buddhists, making no claims to
to be Christians, are one type of witnessing threat to
be dealt with, and perhaps the more manageable. Sectarian Christians claiming Biblical authenticity are another
type, undoubtedly perceived to be more dangerous because
they move within the same basic tradition and, speaking
in seemingly familiar terms, can pass as legitimate until the convert has been beguiled with false doctrine.
Concludes Martin (1977:16):

> Within the theological structure of the cults
> is considerable truth, all of which, it might
> be added, is drawn from Biblical sources, but
> so diluted with human error as to be more dead-
> ly than complete falsehood.

It is for these heretical groups of Judeo-Christian
origins that evangelical authors reserve their most stren-
uous attacks. The comment of Sparks (1977:177) below

on the Children of God, a Jesus movement off-shoot founded
in the 1960s by ex-youth-minister-turned-prophet David
"Moses" Berg, illustrates the venomous extremes which
such rebuttals can reach:

> The blunt truth of the matter is that the Chil-
> dren of God is a bastard orphan heresy. It
> is a bastard because it admits its mother to
> be a whore; an orphan because it pronounces
> its whore-mother dead; and a heresy because
> it has departed from the true teachings of
> the Scripture as those teachings have been
> passed down through the historic Church.

Even direct Satanic inspiration of fringe groups is not
an uncommon allegation. (See, e.g., Bjornstad, 1976:94;
Levitt, 1976:108; Clements, 1975:58.) Yamamoto, of the
Berkeley, California-based Spiritual Counterfeits Project, pulls no punches in The Puppet Master (1977:129)
in attributing the origins of the Unification Church
to infernal powers:

> Moon himself is more deceived than those whom
> he deceives. Moon is not the puppet master,
> Moon is the master puppet. Satan is the puppet
> master.

The published literature decrying "false" sects
and cults stretches back to the earliest colonization
of North America. In the twentieth century alone the
volume of books and articles is staggering. These tracts
fire broadsides at everything from Christian Science/
Seventh Day Adventism/ Mormonism/ Unitarianism/ Humanism/
Spiritualism/ Swedenborgianism to Theosophy and the Jehovah's Witnesses, the Anglo-Israelism of the Armstrongs,
Rosicrucianism, and more recent groups such as the Unification Church and The Way. (See, e.g., Radford, 1913;
Atkins, 1923; Binder, 1933; Spitter, 1962; Clements,
1975; Bjornstad, 1976, 1979; McBeth, 1977; MacCollum,

1978; Enroth, 1979.) The targets of this evangelical onslaught have gradually changed somewhat over the years, of course, as some groups dropped out of the picture and new ones appeared to take their places. For example, no one to my knowledge wastes his breath pouring over Father Divine's alleged blasphemy anymore; attention has now been turned to include Black Muslims, Scientologists, and various mystic groups transplanted from the orient. However, there is a remarkable continuity, not only in the core of sectarian groups (e.g., Mormons, Christian Scientists) who remain under attack but also in the style of refutation. The benchmark against which they are evaluated for "truth", and therefore for ultimate social value, is always a fundamentalist, orthodox interpretation of Christian scriptures. At times the critics can, as Ellwood (1979:xii) notes, "seem inhumanly dispassionate, if not condescending."

THE LIBERAL RESPONSE

Liberal scholars employing a philosophical approach take considerably fewer pains to criticize or refute the doctrines of fringe groups. Instead, they concentrate more on fleshing out the details of the belief, with the unstated, implicit view that these things are worth knowing for their own sakes. One sees little or no Bible quoting in these writings. Nor is there the almost arrogant sense of superiority, the watertight confidence that all spiritual truth has been defined and located, that permeates evangelical sources. That evangelicals and liberals should differ so in the social realities within which they approach the study of fringe religions will come as no surprise to anyone familiar with their respective understandings of Christianity. Nevertheless, reading a non-evangelical philosophical treatment of

fringe groups is a very different experience from reading
any of the books cited in the previous section. It is
like having the fringe group presented for understanding
minus the defensive tension of two adversaries confronting each other. Who can imagine, for example, one of
the evangelical author-critics writing what Charles S.
Braden, a Methodist minister and professor of the history of religion at Northwestern University, says about
his encounters with the personnel of cults such as Psy-
chiana, Unity, and Father Divine's Peace Movement:

> These contacts with the leaders and people
> have been an enriching experience. To have
> known personally such men as Frank B. Robinson,
> Charles Fillmore, Father Divine, and other
> less well-known figures in these movements
> has been a real privilege. (Braden, 1949:xi)

A primary thrust of liberal philosophical writings
on fringe religions is therefore not the attitude expressed in the question, "How can we refute them and
get rid of them?" but rather "Given that they are here,
what sense can we make of them and what effects will
they have on us?" Their presence is not judged a priori
to be a cause for alarm. Change and the evolving nature
of beliefs are accepted facts of religious life to liberals, and as a result they are most concerned to gauge
the potential or actual influence of fringe religious
beliefs on mainline culture. What do these groups offer?
How is it unique? To what extent will it be assimilated?
These questions occupy their research. Thus Marty (1976:
129) foresees positive consequences for American religious culture even if the new religions of the 1970s about
which he writes do not last:

> If the new do not prevail, they will exert
> influences in two ways. One is as an intrusive
> presence, constantly attractive because they

are intrusive and exceptional, an alternative
to or judgement upon majority religion. The
other is as what might be called suffusive
forces; they offer some features that will
suffuse, will cast a glow upon, will subtly
soften or open or alter the Jewish and Christian faiths and the secular style.

Cox (1977), whose book Turning East will be discussed
shortly, also seeks positive elements in the "new orientalism" which, if selected with discrimination, could
infuse Judeo-Christianity with practices and perspectives
at present lacking but ones quite compatible with those
traditions' middle-Asian origins. Judah (1974, 1967)
and Bach (1961) are further examples of this emphasis
on a nonhostile attitude toward fringe groups. Needleman,
in several authored and edited works (Needleman and Baker,
1979; Needleman, 1973, 1972) has tried to locate the
meaning of new religions, particularly those from the
Far East, on the cutting edge of cultural change in western societies. Sensing that for many people the old traditional forms of religion have lost their immediate
relevance, even the churches themselves, he claims, "are
in agony. . . . We see them twisting and turning, seeking to change form without altering their essence."
(1972:9) The appeal of these new belief systems and
groups lies, Needleman concludes, in three important
dimensions of religious experience which they offer and
which have been largely neglected by contemporary western religion:

1. "The Inclusion of the Mind." New religions do
not ignore reason and thought; indeed, they seek
to channel and develop the mind's potential. In
Needleman's words (1972:14): "They bring the idea
that our mind and the power of thought itself is
wretchedly inept without exposure to a spiritual

discipline." But putting the mind back into relig-
ion--balancing it off against the powerful emotional aspects instead of subjugating or repressing
it--is their common goal.

2.   "The Return of the Practical." New religions
return their disciples to the notion of discipline,
whether it be chanting, meditating, fasting, or
outward manifestations of obedience, commitment
and humility (e.g., shaved heads, saffron robes,
ascetic lifestyles) that so shock outsiders. The
instrumental side of religion, Needleman claims,
has been lost in western religion. (He qualifies
this point by noting that western convents and monasteries still provide such discipline; mainline
denominations and congregations, however, obviously
do not.)

3.   "The Modern Underestimation of Man." New religions do not share the pessimism of traditional religious forms about mankind's inability to lift
its spiritual condition through its own efforts.
Modern psychology (particularly of the psychoanalytic type) has reinforced this religious view and
thus effectively "reduced" our concept of human
potential in religion.

I would not argue that either the liberals or the
evangelicals bring to their concern with philosophical
matters any greater personal bias or assumptive baggage
than researchers locked into the social realities of
other perspectives. One can make defensible judgments
as to the utility of given perspectives and variations
within perspectives, however, because the information
one obtains about any fringe religion is directly related to the approach of study taken. Insofar as both the
evangelical and liberal scholars desire descriptive information about fringe religions, their viewpoints probably have equal utility. However, from that point on

they diverge in what else they want to know and why (and
then utility resides in the eye of the reader). The evangelicals desire systematic refutation for obvious reasons. They are committed to a world view in which fin-
ite, definable truth is perceived to be under seige by
forces inherently opposed to truth. For that reason their
research reports are polemical exercises in defending
orthodox Christianity. Liberals, on the other hand, are
less committed to the details of orthodox Christianity
and more apt to accord some degree of legitimacy to all
sincere religious inspiration. The threat to their own
orientation is understandably less. Because of this,
they tend to emphasize in a more constructive, eclectic
fashion what further insights can be gained from new
religious groups.

Otherwise, the final distinction between the two
types of philosophical research that always strikes me
is one of style. The polemical concerns of the evangelical authors lend their writings a flavor that is tense,
defensive, critical, at times even vicious. The liberals
adopt a more moderate tone, with much less of a tendency
to disparage.

CASE STUDIES

The two case studies below follow the evangelical-
liberal division which I have outlined above. Walter
R. Martin's The Kingdom of the Cults is a classic survey
of the "core heresies" about which evangelicals have
been concerned in this century. Others, generally less
thorough, have tried to imitate Martin, but his work
remains the standard. Harvey Cox's more recent Turning
East is a much different book, seeking a new synthesis

of eastern practices and Christianity that will revitalize the latter. Both works are the products of competent
scholars attempting to come to grips with the theologi-
ical implications of fringe religions.

FIRST CASE

The Kingdom of the Cults
Walter R. Martin

Walter Martin, as the book jacket of The Kingdom
of the Cults proclaims, is a well educated, prolific
author and articulate spokesperson for the evangelical
view of fringe religions. Possessing both a master's
degree and a doctorate in comparative religion, he has
written over a dozen books and numerous articles. For
over a decade he was a regular participant on a popular
nationally broadcast radio talk show and also hosted
his own program at one time. He is an ordained Baptist
minister. He is also professor of Biblical theology and
comparative religion at the Melodyland School of Theology at Anaheim, California and founder/director of
the Christian Research Institute. (In the modern anti-
cult movement he is also active as a lecturer and re-
corder of cassette tape lectures.)

The Kingdom of the Cults critiques the "Big Three"
sectarian Christian organizations which upset evangelical Christians the most: the Jehovah's Witnesses, the
Christian Scientists, and the Mormons. In addition it
considers the Peace Movement of Father Divine, Spiritualism, groups of oriental inspiration such as Theosophy
and Zen Buddhism, Swedenborgianism, Bahaism, Black Muslims, the Armstrong's World Wide Church of God, and the
Unity School of Christianity. In an appendix he also

covers Seventh-Day Adventism, Unitarianism, and the various forms of Rosicrucianism. This interesting assortment of groups represents a laundry list of major Christian sects (and non-Christian) that preoccupied evangelicals when the book was first printed in 1965. It had its twenty fourth printing and a revision in 1977, but none of the newer controversial "cults" involved in the deprogramming controversy, such as the Unification Church or the Children of God, were included. Had Martin included them in his later editions he would have had a longer table of contents and would not have had to include refutations of Father Divine (who died in 1965, his movement effectively folding up soon after) or the tiny following of Swedenborgianism. Nevertheless, despite the book's lack of consideration of some of the more recent fringe religious arrivals, Kingdom has been a staple on the reading lists of anti-cult books and sources that are circulated in the network of the current anti-cult movement.

When Martin first wrote this book he obviously was interested in taking on what he perceived to be the major fringe religions of the 1960s, whether Christian heresies or foreign imports (how else to explain the inclusion of Zen Buddhism—a fringe group in the United States but a major conventional denomination in Japan —and the Black Muslims, neither of which makes any pretense at being Christian?). He also has a "hidden agenda" of other social movements of which he does not approve that becomes apparent occasionally in his theological discussions. In his summary of Zen, for example, he devotes part of a page (234) to castigating the pseudo-intellectuals in the United States who, "ceaselessly mouthing fragmented sentences, liberally sprinkled with symbolic language, Zen terminology and fractured logic," feed their egos and merely seek publicity. There is a strong feeling one gets that Martin was experiencing the rather common middle-class shock at beatniks and the emerging counter-culture of the 1960s. He seems to resent particularly the attention they received in such magazines as Time and Newsweek. When Martin is on non-Christian turf his prejudices are also more visible. Summing up Zen Buddhism as primarily a doctrine of self-love, he maintains that it breeds a lack of spiritual and social responsibility and directly contributes to major socio-economic problems. In an incredible statement of ethnocentrism he writes: "For in almost every area of the world where Buddhism of any form holds sway, there stalks the spectre of disease, hunger, and moral and spiritual decay." (240) Martin obviously did not have in mind the miserable living conditions of many populations in the Christian dictatorships of South America. He also writes that orientals are "slaves to their religions," thereby concluding his analysis of Zen Buddhism with an innuendo that can perhaps be regarded as a primitive precursor of the "mind control/brainwashing" argument that flowered among anti-cult groups in the 1970s.

More than most writers of this genre, Martin goes to some effort not only to discuss openly his own Christian perspective with readers but to admit that beyond mere refutaiton of heresies he wants "to familiarize the reader with the refreshing truths of the Gospel of Christ, that he may see the great heritage which is ours in the Christian faith, and be challenged both to more effectively live and to witness for the Savior." (16) He also prefaces his discussions of the various groups with several chapters, one addressing the problems of theological terms being used inconsistently in the different doctrines and Biblical passages frequently being used out of context and misinterpreted.[2] Another chapter

entitled "The Psychological Structure of Cultism" examines Martin's allegations that cult members, regardless of their particular group, are psychologically different from nonmembers, not so much with regard to
their personalities before they joined but in terms of
their states of mind as cult members. They are, Martin
claims, close-minded and personally antagonistic to nonmembers. Martin attributes this dogmatism to the structures of their elitest theologies and isolated organizations. He is not inherently opposed to such qualities,
however. In a statement of refreshing candor not often
found in evangelical writings but one which unfortunately leads Martin into psychological reductionism, he
writes (26):

> We do not wish to imply that there is no such
> thing as an authoritative dogmatism which is
> valid and true (such as the teachings of Jesus
> Christ), but rather that cult systems tend
> to invest with the authority of the superna-
> tural whatever pronouncements are deemed ne-
> cessary to condition and control the minds
> of the faithful.

The last four of the book's nineteen chapters anal-
yze the activities of "cults" in world missions, the
image of Jesus portrayed in their doctrines, cult evan-
gelism in American society, and suggestions for how such
fringe groups can be more effectively combatted, respectively. Many of these last measures have in fact come
to pass with the foundation during the 1970s of anti-
cult coalitions by many evangelical and conservative
church groups and the growth of anti-cult mission groups
such as the Spiritual Counterfeits Project in Berkeley,
California, and Martin's own Christian Research Institute.

As encyclopedic as Martin attempts to be in The Kingdom of the Cults, I doubt very seriously that any of the groups represented would consider his treatments of them as anything other than caricatures. Martin's basic purpose is, after all, not to understand them beyond the point of being able to refute them. His serious scholarship is still only meant to be a tool to further the propagation of a particular brand of Christianity and not an end in itself.

SECOND CASE

Turning East
Harvey Cox

Harvey Cox, Harvard Divinity School professor and liberal theological author, states in the beginning of Turning East's final chapter:

> We need an authentic contemporary form of spir-
> ituality. We must find it, I believe, in our
> own tradition, not somewhere else. (157)

These two sentences illustrate, respectively, his assumption before he began his study of neo-oriental groups in modern society, and his conclusion about their possible contributions to his ideal of a revitalized Christianity. Turning East is a very different study from The Kingdom of the Cults. Far from assuming a canonical permanent orthodoxy that is relevant to all times and peoples, Cox views traditional Christian belief as outmoded and functionally stagnant. Therefore he does not treat the new wave of oriental doctrines and groups pouring into the United States during the 1960s and 1970s as a threat. Rather, he, like many others, "turns east" to discover what remedies different religious traditions might offer aging, senile Christianity.

Turning East represents a continuation of Cox's search to construct a more experiential satisfying Christianity that is compatible with modern urban industrial society, a search that can be traced back through The Seduction of the Spirit (1973) and his other earlier works. He sometimes has referred to his goal as a "people's religion". In his view it would not be a mammoth bureaucracy run in corporate fashion as are many denominations, wtih its interpretation of sin and social policy managed as the monopoly of a professional clerical elite. Nor would it be packaged for the media with the superficial cliches, glitter and hype imposed by modern electronics. It would emphasize direct experience with the transcendent, a firsthand confrontation with the supernatural that would easily and more effectively supplant our presently remote knowledge of such things. It would be an authentic religion in that it would infuse itself across institutional boundaries and not compartmentalize spirituality apart from what we now regard as the secular world.

Cox explored the multitudinous varieties of neooriental religions dotting the American scene during the 1970s to see firsthand what he might learn from them to help in the reconstruction of Christianity. As Cox notes, this new interest in oriental religions is itself not typical of previous intellectual infatuations with Eastern ideas in American history. Rather, in this new era many persons other than academics and intellectuals are involved in these groups, and moreover they are more interested in the practices--the acting out--of the religious belief than in specific doctrines.

He began participating in the smorgasboard of sects and cults to be found in his own locale of Cambridge, Massachusetts, or Benares-on-the-Charles as he called it. He meditated, chanted, performed yoga and Tai Chi,

got high on Peyote: all in an attempt to go beyond mere
objective observation and enter into empathic understanding of why persons joined these groups. He freely admits
that in the end his search for a possible spiritual essence which he could bring back to his Christianity led
him to commit the methodological taboo avoided by social
scientists: he "went native" and "turned east":

> Then something I had not anticipated happened.
>
> I discovered that when someone is studying
> beehives up close, regardless of how much in-
> ner distance is retained, there is still a
> distinct possibility that the investigator
> can be stung. . . . Almost without noticing
> what was happening, I slipped across the bor-
> der between them and us. (14)

Contrary to his own fears, Cox discovered that this
change of perspective made him more, not less, critical
of his new oriental milieu and sharpened his discrimination of what aspects of their religious practices, minus
foreign trappings could perhaps be of value to a revamp-
ed Christianity. As a result, he found that his formal
studies in the classical doctrines of Eastern religions
were of little use in understanding these groups; they
are more "neo" than "oriental". The book's most interesting example is Cox's discovery that meditation can
be a useful technique for periodically "recharging" energies in a fast-paced, computerized society, and Cox
develops an analogue between it and the Hebrew concept
of Sabbath in the Old Testament. The ancient Jews by
law were forbidden to work on the Sabbath, a practice
that permitted everyone in the society to simply rest
and reintegrate themselves away from the daily pressures
of business and survival. It was functional then for
their society just as meditation can contribute something to ours, Cox maintains. He refers to the Sabbath
as the Biblical equivalent of meditation and conversely

to meditation as the possible modern equivalent of Sabbath. What else can we use to fill its place in a secular society where Sunday has become a day to run errands
and where retail stores do not close and it is "business
as ususal?"

Much of neo-orientalism will be of little help,
Cox concludes. Our western tendency to psychologize and
our concern with the individual self almost invariably
leads us into narcissism. (Perhaps William Martin, in
the First Case, could not distinquish between the nar-
cissistic neo-Zen he saw and the authentic selfless Zen
of Japanese traditions.) While Buddhism can help us detach from shallow desires, materialism, and much pain,
we will also have to detach from loving relationships
--a price too high to pay and incompatible with our own
Biblical traditions. Cox repeatedly asked persons why
they had "turned east" and, not unexpectedly, received
an array of replies. Some sought greater harmony with
nature or a sense of community; others were closer to
Cox in his sense of a need to directly experience the
transcendent. In rejecting the exotic veneer of these
groups, Cox concludes of the participants: "The East
Turners do not represent a way out of our Western spiritual crises. But they do help us understand it much
better." (103)

Cox's solution to revitalize Christianity is to
create direct experience, to live as the first generation Christians did when they lacked a rigid tradition
and slavish concern with spiritual references. We need
to stop reading about God and confront His Presence--
as we ourselves construct our understanding of that Pres-
ence--directly. It would not mean taking off on some
strange tangent based on an obscure interpretation of
a Bible verse, like the modern Garbage Eater, but rather a return to a concern for direct experience. We can

learn from studying the struggles of the First Century Christians preserved in their correspondence and history. They lived in a pre-Christian world; we live in a post-Christian one. Neither of us, they and we, had or have very clear guidelines.

It goes without saying that Cox's evident sympathy for the groups and persons he discusses in Turning East and his dismissal of orthodox Biblical Christianity both make his entire approach anathema to evangelicals. From their perspective he glorifies paganism and rejects the Death and Resurrection of Jesus Christ and the fulfillment of mankind's covenant with God. His willingness to endorse mental and spiritual discipline and the fact that he takes these groups' religious goals at face value also earn him no praise from anti-cult proponents who maintain that these gurus are all con-men and their followers all "brainwashed". There is much in Cox's tentative solution to our alleged spiritual crisis in the West that is vague and undeveloped because Cox is still working through the solution. I say "alleged" spiritual crisis because I believe it is a highly debatable point to claim that any age is uniquely one of spiritual crisis. What we may be reading in Turning East, after all is said and done, is an articulate introspective look at Cox's own spiritual crisis and the crises of similar persons but not necessarily any culture-wide breakdown in Christian faith. Neo-oriental fringe groups have not drawn in the majority of Americans or had much widespread appeal, and during the same decade that college students were blissfully chanting mantras at Benares-on-the-Charles the fundamentalist Biblical churches with their "stagnant" message grew steadily in membership with persons more than eager to proclaim their satisfaction with their faith. Finally, I think one could question the intellectual capabilities or patience of most persons to engage

in anything as profoundly tenuous and arduous as fash-
ioning a viable new faith. It is fine for ambitious cosmopolitan Harvard Divinity School professors, but I doubt
the majority of Christians either can or want to undertake such a task.

NOTES

[1] As David Bromley and I have argued in our analysis
of the religious institution's participation in the current anti-cult movement (Shupe and Bromley, 1980; Chapter Two), religious belief systems (whatever their adherents' claims otherwise) are inherently nonempirical
from a scientific standpoint. Their validity cannot be
verified with data. Religions depend instead upon con-
sistency--that their fundamental tenets be considered
immutable truths and applicable universally, that believers' subjective spiritual experiences become testimonies and reinforce one another. The more closely a
group's doctrines serve as guides for daily behavior,
the more critical consistency becomes. Consistency can
be eroded by religious pluralism (that results often
in a plurality of lifestyles as well) and therefore the
two--the need for consistency and religious pluralism
--tend usually to exist in a state of tension.
[2] Martin feels that the "semantic game" is a standard feature of cultic groups, one that they deliberately play to mislead naive Christians. Therein, he claims,
lies the similarity of cultism to communism which also
"plays a type of hypnotic music upon a semantic harp
of terminological deception" (19)

REFERENCES

Atkins, Gaius G. 1923. Modern Religious Cults and Movements. New York: Fleming H. Revell.

Bach, Marcus. 1961. Strange Sects and Curious Cults. New York: Dodd and Mead.

Bjornstad, James. 1976. The Moon is not the Son. Minneapolis: Bethany Fellowship.

_____. 1979. Counterfeits at Your Door. Glendale, CA: Regal Books.

Binder, Louis Richard. 1933. Modern Religious Cults and Society. New York: AMS Press.

Braden, Charles S. 1949. These Also Believe. New York: The MacMillan Company.

Clements, R.D. 1975. God and the Gurus. Downers Grove, IL: Inter-Varsity Press.

Coser, Lewis. 1956. The Functions of Social Conflict. New York: The Free Press.

Cox, Harvey. 1977. Turning East. New York: Simon and Schuster.

_____. 1973. The Seduction of the Spirit. New York: Simon and Schuster.

Davies, Horton. 1972. Christian Deviations. (Third Revised Edition) Philadelphia: The Westminster Press.

Elwood, Jr., Robert S. 1979. Alternative Altars: Unconventional and Eastern Spirituality in America. Chicago: University of Chicago Press.

_____. 1974. The Eagle and the Rising Sun: Americans and the New Religions of Japan. Philadelphia: The Westminister Press.

Enroth, Ronald. 1979. The Lure of the Cults. Chappaqua, NY: Christian Herald Books.

Judah, J. Stillson. 1974. "The Hare Krishna Movement." Pp. 463-78 in Irving I. Zaretsky and Mark P. Leone, eds., Religious Movements in Contemporary America. Princeton, NJ: Princeton University Press.

_____. 1967. The History and Philosophy of Metaphysical Movements in America. Philadelphia: The Westminster Press.

Levitt, Zola. 1976. The Spirit of Sun Myung Moon. Irvine, CA: Harvest House.

MacCollum, Joel. 1979. The Way of Victor Paul Wierwille. New York: The Seabury Press.

McBeth, L. 1977. Strange New Religions. (Revised Edition) Nashville: Broadman Press.

McFarland, H. Neill. 1967. The Rush Hour of the Gods. New York: MacMillan.

Martin, Walter R. 1977. The Kingdom of the Cults. Minneapolis: Bethany Fellowship.

Marty, Martin E. 1976. A Nation of Behavers. Chicago: University of Chicago Press.

Needleman, Jacob. 1973. "Winds from the East: Youth & Counter Culture." Pp. 78-83 in Edward F. Heenan ed., Mystery, Magic, and Miracle: Religion in a Post-Aquarian Age. Englewood Cliffs, NJ: Prentice-Hall.

_____. 1972. The New Religions. New York: Pocketbooks.

Needleman, Jacob and George Baker, eds., 1978. Understanding the New Religions. New York: The Seabury Press.

Offner, Clark B. and Henry Van Straelen. 1963. Modern Japanese Religions. New York: Twayne Publishers.

Radford, Lewis. 1913. Ancient Heresies in Modern Dress. Melbourne: Robertson.

Sparks, Jack. 1977. The Mind Benders. New York: Thomas Nelson.

Spittler, Russell P. 1962. Cults and Isms: Twenty Alternatives to Evangelical Christianity. Grand Rapids, MI: Baker Book House.

Starkes, M. Thomas. 1972. Confronting the Popular Cults.
    Nashville: Broadman Press.
Van Baalen, J.K. 1938. The Chaos of Cults. Grand Rapids,
    MI: Erdmanns.
Yamamoto, J.I., 1977. The Puppet Master. Downers Grove,
    IL: Inter-Varsity Press.

SUGGESTED FURTHER READING

Breese, David. 1979. Know the Marks of Cults. Wheaton,
    IL: Victor Books.
Bjornstad, James. 1976. The Transcendental Mirage.
    Minneapolis: Bethany Press.
Capps, Walter H. 1978. "The Interpretation of New Re-
    ligion and Religious Studies" Pp. 101-12 in Jacob
    Needleman and George Baker, eds., Understanding
    the New Religions. New York: The Seabury Press.
Langford, H. 1977. Traps: A Probe of Those Strange New
    Cults. Montgomery, AL: Committee for Christian Edu-
    cation and Publications, Presbyterian Church in
    America.
MacCollum, Joel. 197 . Carnival of Souls. New York: The
    Seabury Press.
Means, Pat. 1976. The Mystical Maze. Downers Grove, IL:
    Campus Crusade for Christ.
Streiker, Lowell D. 1978. The Cults Are Coming.
    Nashville: Abingdon.

THOUGHTS FOR FURTHER CONSIDERATION

The polar opposite reactions of evangelical and liberal philosophers to fringe religions illustrate about as clearly as any example could how the social meaning of a phenomenon is a product of expectations and assumptions. Clearly the meaning of fringe groups is in the eye of the beholder and not inherent. But is there a middle ground between Cox and Martin? Could not the "new orientalism" help shed light on, or give new significance to, modern Biblical faith (itself an oriental product)? Can the tension that I suggested in Note Two may be inevitable between religious fundamentalism and religious pluralism be constructively channelled into maintaining a faith tradition rather than resulting in abandoning or redesigning it?

THE ANTHROPOLOGICAL PERSPECTIVE

When anthropologists study fringe religious groups they focus on the latters' rituals, beliefs, and general practices as indices of broader social change. This interpretation follows directly from the common anthropological assumption about the primary function which religion provides for people sharing the same culture; namely, that religion is a set of interrelated sacred symbols that explain their physical and social worlds. Through placing value on arrived-at agreements about status, power, responsibilities and reciprocities, and other patterns of human organization, religion infuses the daily world of people's experience with legitimacy and meaning--how did it come to be? How does it operate? Why are its rules sovereign and to be preserved? Why is it preferable to other alternatives? (See, Geertz, 1966, 1958.) In the abstract case, as society undergoes gradual transitions in its structure over time religion likewise accommodates to pressures for updating its relevancy with its own complementary changes. However, when changes in society are abrupt and discontinuous, such as in times of revolution, civil war, wide-spread natural disasters, or colonial takeover by a very dissimilar culture, the traditional religion has little or no opportunity to adapt to the radically new social conditions. It then offers inadequate explanations for the transformed daily experience. As a result, many people outside the old religious establishment set about generating a more viable set of sacred meanings and/or are highly responsive to receiving them. The new meanings constructed by these religious movements, as known in their beliefs and practices, are linked to the new social conditions by anthropologists. Indeed, proponents of the anthropological perspective assume the social and the sacred to be so closely related that change in the former must almost invariably cause change in the latter. (See, Eister, 1974.) Thus on two levels--in the "content" of beliefs and practices of specific groups, and in the sheer "frequency of appearance of such religious regeneration movements--fringe groups presumably serve as barometers or indices of social change. (For example, incidences of witchcraft accusations are considered by anthropologists to represent the presence of strains in communities--see, Marwick, 1970.)

REVITALIZATION MOVEMENTS

This line of analysis of fringe religions has been developed most fully by Anthony F.C. Wallace in his concept of revitalization movements. Such movements represent, in his words (Wallace, 1956:265) "a deliberate, organized, conscious effort by members of a society to construct a more satisfying culture." Faced with the inescapable, irrefutable destruction of their former way of life, a people will search for a cosmic or religious scheme that simultaneously explains their fall from a happier state in a previous era to their present straits and gives a theory of hope for better times. Wallace sees such revitalization efforts as normal, periodic occurences in every society's religion(s):

> In the revitalization model, the religious
> institutions of a society are seen as passing
> more or less regularly, over the generations,
> through a cycle of revitalization, stabiliza-
> tion, and decline. (1966:36)

A vibrant, responsive religion expands (perhaps aggressively), settles into maintaining a status quo equilbri-
um with its secular counterpart institutions, and then,
whether by outside intervention or sheer weight of cultural inertia, declines either quickly or slowly. Such
a cyclical model is similar to Max Weber's concept of
the role of charisma in the sociology of religion. Weber
(1964a, 1964b) saw religions founded by initially dyna-
mic, original charismatic leaders; then their personal
charisma is lost over succeeding generations as the cult
expands into the corporate bureaucracy of a church, and
finally a breakaway sectarian movement response to the
rigid objectification of dogma and perceived spiritual
bankruptcy of the church occurs which begins the cycle
anew.

Wallace regards as a classic example of a revitalization movement the "Good Message" cult of the Iroquois
Indians, begun by a Seneca chief named Handsome Lake in
1799. The Iroquois in the eighteenth century had entered
into a dark state of steady decline and social disorganization. Having lost much of their power when the British won hegemony over North America following the French
and Indian War, they subsequently sank into further woes
when they incurred the Americans' enmity by having sided
with the British during the American Revolution. During
the latter years their homes and fields had been razed,
their lands taken by whites. Iroquois tribes and families began to disintegrate within a generation on their
inadequate reservations,while disease, infant mortality,
and alcoholism ravaged their dwindling numbers. In 1799
Handsome Lake, himself an alcoholic and raised as a child
by Quakers, began receiving prophetic visions from the
Great Spirit via spirit messengers. These spirits told
Handsome Lake to found the New Religion of the Iroquois
(the Gai'Wiio, or "Good Message") and reform his breth-
ren. They were to abstain from alcohol, attend white

Quaker schools and become literate, engage diligently
in agriculture (and never sell their lands), abandon
witchcraft and all paganism except for selected fertil-
ity festivals connected with the growing season, and
perhaps most important, maintain strong, racially pure
familial bonds (miscegenation was forbidden). Handsome
Lake's revitalized monotheism restored morality and
cohesion to the Iroquois tribes. Their social disintegration stabilized, reversed itself, and finally prosperity replaced it. After 180 years the religion is still
practiced (in several sectarian forms) among modern Iroquois Indians.

     Revitalization movements, sometimes under different
labels such as "nativistic", "messianic" or "millenarian" have been widely researched in anthropology. The
Ghost Dance movement which spread rapidly throughout
the Plains Indians tribes in the late nineteenth century
was only one famous instance. For example, General George
A. Custer, at the Battle of the Little Big Horn, met
up with its followers under the leadership of their famous Sioux high priest-warrior Sitting Bull, (see, La
Barre, 1972; Mooney, 1965.) Others include the sudden
flowering of "new religions" following World War II in
both Japan (the Shinko Shukyo--Norbeck, 1970; Ikado,
1968; McFarland, 1967; Thomsen, 1963) and South Korea
(the Shinhung Jonggyo--Moos, 1967, 1964; Syn-duk, 1967),
some nineteenth century Polynesian movements (Burridge,
1969), and their twentieth century counterparts in Africa
(Lanternari, 1963:19-62).

CARGO CULTS

     The best known form of revitalization movement is
undoubtedly the cargo cult. Actually the term "cargo
cult" refers not to one specific historical movement

but rather to a generic type of religious innovation that everywhere arises in response to the same general societal conditions. Variations of the cargo cult can be found worldwide, but the first observed examples came from those areas of Melanesia which were European colonies in the early part of this century. Briefly, a cargo cult movement possesses the following essential features:

A colonized native population finds its traditional culture and way of life abruptly shattered by the white foreign invasion. Political sovereignty is usurped by the provincial government, the economy is radically transformed from simple agricultural farming/fishing into one that is organized around exporting the country's raw materials using the natives as cheap labor, and missionaries, imported to "civilize" the indigenous population, thoroughly discredit the old gods and beliefs. In a less differentiated society in which religion is far more integrated into daily affairs and institutions, the sum effect is to transform the natives into marginal persons. They are barred from the governmental bureaucracy except in menial positions of low responsibility. (Suffrage is out of the question.) Their role in the economy is simply as low-paid manual labor with little hope for improvement. Even in the whites' religion they remain second-class citizens.

Out of this unhappy state emerges a charismatic prophet, one who claims a vision, dream, or revelation. His message most often reflects the blocked aspirations of the natives and, as Burridge (1969) and Washington (1973) observe, includes explicit themes of power. It involves a syncretistic blend of both native and Christian ideas but (in its original version) invariably fixates on two common elements: the "cargo" in the foreigner's ships, and the natives' own ancestors. The cargo is last seen by the natives as raw materials before it

eventually "returns" as desirable consumer goods that
only the white colonists can possess. From the natives'
point of view the mysterious transmutation of raw materials into finished goods takes place in holds of the
ships--often assumed to be performed by spirits or the
natives' dead ancestors. The cargo takes on primary symbolic significance. As Lanternari (1963:166) notes, "The
'cargo' is identified by the natives with their European
masters, both as tangible evidence of their wealth and
as symbol of their mastery." The ancestors play a key
role in the cult since the day is believed imminent when
they will return on the ships and redistribute the goods
to the natives. Sometimes there is to be a coordinated
uprising between ancestors in their realm and the natives
in theirs; sometimes natural calamities (earthquakes,
floods, and so forth) will wipe away whites and anyone
not subscribing to the cult's doctrines before the ships
arrive; sometimes the specific version may be more purely
nativistic and dictate not only a revolt but also total
destruction of the whites' goods and material culture.
(See Lanternari, 1963, 161-90; Worsely, 1957; Williams,
1934.) In every case, however, the cargo cult is a broad
rejection of colonial political and cultural subjugation
which an innovative religious cosmology legitimates.

    Analogues to the Melanesian variety can be found
elsewhere. For example, the Ghost Dance cult, which played such an important role in the North American Indian
Wars of the late nineteenth century, began with the vision of an Indian named Wodziwob in 1869. The faithful
were to dance and sing in appointed ways until a great
cataclysm would occur. Thereupon the whites would be
swallowed up in an earthquake (leaving, however, their
material goods and buildings for the Indians to use)
and--in an understandable twist on the Melanesian ver-
sion--the Indians' ancestors would all return riding

a railroad train instead of ships. (See, Lanternari, 1963:113-14; Mooney, 1965.)

The cargo cult phenomenon is worth considering for reasons other than that it is simply a widespread, predictable occurence in underdeveloped and colonized cultures. More importantly for our purposes, the cargo cult has become an important anthropological model for understanding fringe religions in places other than New Guinea, Africa, and nineteenth century North America. As the two case studies in this chapter should indicate, the assumptions that are part of the cargo model are frequently carried over when it is applied as a general perspective elsewhere and need to be analyzed critically. This is especially true since the cargo cult model has been appropriated wholesale by scholars in other social sciences. (See, e.g., Yinger, 1963.)

The basic anthropological understanding of fringe religions, following the cargo cult model, is that they serve as "bridges" to help many persons make the transition between periods of cultural stability or during times of particularly disorienting social change. One should recall the basic anthropological assumption that there are ubiquitous, persistent needs for supernatural explanations to integrate life's experiences into a coherent meaning. Characteristically a wave of broad social change which transforms or seriously weakens traditional institutions, including established religion, results in a period of crisis. Conventional religion, whose assumed function is to buffer persons from anxieties of life and to offer solace, proves to be inadequate for some persons and must be replaced, albeit temporarily with bizarre substitutes.

One of the most important, but often implicit, assumptions of this approach, is that such revitalizing groups attract the emotionally unstable and individuals unable to cope with the pressures of social change on their own. This perception is not surprising. The first reports of cargo cults phenomena by Williams (e.g., 1934) referred to it as "a madness," and a number of early cargo cult prophets in Melanesia were even committed to insane asylums (Lanternari, 1963:171). They were, after all, posing social threats with their revolutionary visions, and by the standards of early observers--persons who presumably made some common-sense assumptions about what are "true" as opposed to "false" religions--these emergent prophets did seem "crazy". In my own readings of reports of cargo cult-type religions I have found few reports of any length that did not include detailed evidence to show that the founder had a borderline personality. Perhaps many did, but it is an easy move to infer next the psychological states of persons who would be attracted to such bizarre doctrines and leadership --though this constitutes a scientifically inappropriate jump from cultural data to psychological inference. Wallace (1966:34) is aware of this psychological assumption in his revitalization theory. He notes, "it recognizes the integrative power of religious experience for the distraught and disillusioned individual in search of salvation." To demonstrate that members of such groups are disillusioned and distraught requires empirical support; otherwise it is armchair psychology.

In "The Social Psychological Perspective" we will examine the theoretical tradition of social psychology known as "deprivation theory" that emphasizes the presumably problematic, even psychopathological motives of converts to "weird" or nonconventional religions, and also the growing body of research findings that dispute it. Real pathology, and not merely suspicion of it from observations of socially "different" behavior, is, after all, an empirical matter. I do not suggest that it never exists. I am also mindful, however, that even McFarland (1967), who takes a cargo cult interpretation of the new religions suddenly burgeoning in Japan's chaotic post-World Warr II society, notes (87) various other causes of "cult" membership, such as earnest employers and superiors in secular relationships pressuring subordinates and juniors into joining (at least nominally) various groups to which the former belonged--motives which have little to do with problematic psychological states. Here I want mainly to observe that the assumption that the early cargo cults attracted those least emotionally stable in the native populations has been carried over in the general tendency to view participants in groups like the Black Muslims, the Hare Krishnas, the Unification Church, and segments of the Jesus movement as having had, previous to their membership, significant problems different from those of the general population or at least decreased abilities to deal with such problems. When such an assumption goes untested, the validity of the entire perspective that such fringe groups serve as "bridges" for weaker individuals to weather social change can be jeopardized. It can become a subtle temptation for personal bias to translate unconsciously into "objective analysis".

A second important assumption in this perspective is that while there may exist some perennial "underworld" or permanent subculture of "esoteric", deviant religion (as Triyakian [1972] suggests), significant numbers of new fringe religions are produced by the powerful social forces running rampant during times of extraordinarily fast or widespread change. Indeed, Wallace (1966:30) concludes that, following the logic of his revitalization theory, religious beliefs and practices always find

their origins in such problematic social conditions.
It is an undeniable fact that veritable floods of fringe
religions have been observed to emerge during particular
times of rapid social change--though Wallace has undoubtedly overstated the case. Norbeck (1970:11) for
example, cites the figures of 720 new religious sects
in postwar Japan in 1951. By the mid-1960s there were
still 404 in existence.

However, the cargo cult model is very vague as to
what constitutes a "time of significant, tumultuous
change." There is little disagreement that the post-World
War II orient would qualify, but what about the United
States during the early 1970s when a number of fringe
religious groups suddenly enjoyed growth spurts? Were
the 1970s suddenly "hot-bed" years of discontent and
radical social transition as compared to the "quieter"
1960s (when most groups such as the Unification Church,
which had been in the United States since 1959, had only
modest membership)? Obviously the explanation is more
complex than simply designating the 1970s as "a time
of rapid change." The decade of the 1960s witnessed a
shift in the world view of much of a youthful generation
brought on partly by international events (a controversial war, to name one), crises at home (civil rights,
student and environmental concerns, assassinations, to
name a few), and economic trends in corporate capitalism
building since at least World War II. No serious observer would claim that the 1960s did not constitute
a period of significant social upheaval. Clearly the
types of change in the two decades were not the same.
The 1970s were more propitious to religious movements
than the prior decade had been for a constellation of
reasons considerably more complicated than simply saying
these were years of radical change. (See Bromley and
Shupe, 1979:57-95; Foss and Larkin, 1979.) And given

the small number of persons relative to the total population who joined these groups, one might also question how much seriously disorienting change occurred. White (1964) and other historians have challenged the notion that certain centuries or periods are marked by change while others are not. White's survey of technological progress in so-called stable, static medieval European society casts doubt on the validity of the change/no-change distinction.

But even granting that some periods can be isolated as times of extraordinary sudden change, which I think is feasible, a limitation in the cargo cult model is its preoccupation with the questions of WHY DO THESE GROUPS ORIGINATE? and WHO JOINS THEM? Rather than simply disappearing when the formative period of rapid change is ended, many groups survive, e.g., 56 per cent of Japan's new religions did, using Norbeck's figures above, and some even go on to prosper. This fact throws doubt on the whole notion of understanding these fringe groups merely as transitory "bridges", whatever they once meant to their original members. McFarland alluded to this problem when he wrote, in the mid-1960s, about Japan's postwar religion boom:

> Now . . . two decades after the end of the war, there are reasons for asking whether the "rush hour of the gods" may not prove to be a period of considerable long-range significance in the religious and social history of Japan. (1967:5)

The basic anthropological assumption that the religious institutions of societies must at least periodically regenerate themselves in order to come to moral grips with significant nonreligious changes is an enormously important one. It takes the frequent occurence of emerging fringe religions out of the realm of amusing oddities and redefines them as "normal" phenomena worth taking seriously. As such it is one of the fundamental cornerstones of a comparative scientific approach to religion. It helps lend an integrative perspective to such disparate groups as the new religions of Japan and Korea (discussed above), the millenarian movements of North American Indians (see Lanternari, 1963:63-132), and the Jamaican Rastafarians (see Barrett, 1977; 1974: 153-202). At the same time readers do well to keep in mind the origins of much of the research on revitalization movements, in particular on cargo cults. Such studies were generally conducted in a specific type of third world society: technologically primitive, politically subordinated and therefore intensely frustrated, often racially discriminated against, suffering widespread social disorganization and left with the choice of (1) a discredited impotent indigenous religious tradition, (2) a foreign, often condescending faith, or (3) some more satisfying, innovative third alternative. Religious alternatives that begin in a more urbane, industrialized, noninvaded, religiously pluralistic culture, the traditional religious institution(s) of which has/have simply "gone flat" and irresponsive rather than been overwhelmed, may not be able to be lumped together analytically with the former type of revitalization movements. For example, not only their chances of survival but also their perspectives of the larger social order (e.g., in need of total replacement versus limited reform) should logically differ.

We must also recall the assumption commonly made that fringe religions arising in such oppressed third-world situations represent earnest attempts to comprehend radical social change by persons who are either strongly religiously predisposed or incapable of responding successfully without the emotional crutch of messianic/millenarian/nativistic expectations, i.e.,

that for reasons of psychological inadequacy they require the revitalization movement as a coping mechanism
to help them "bridge" the tumultuous seas of transition.
That certain eras are especially marked by rapid change
creating a special set of dynamics for the emergence
of fringe groups is tenable but also easily overgeneralized. All times are times of social change, and fringe
groups are ubiquitous. The burden of proof to demonstrate a unique milieu and an extraordinary increase
in fringe groups is on the researcher. So also is the
responsibilty to provide evidence that these fringe
groups really do attract the "down-and-outers", the persons with weak egos, or the mutually distraught and con-
fused.

Finally, if there is one deep-laden theme in much
of the revitalization/cargo cult literature that lurks
between the lines and presupposes another entire set
of assumptions about human nature, it is that human be-
ings--or at least particularly weak-willed or dispriv-
ileged ones--are more or less the passive victims of
social change. Wallace's revitalization theory acknowl-
edges that persons engage in revitalizing religion to
create a more relevant moral meaning for their world.
This can be nothing other than a positive, constructive
effort. Yet in much research on Melanesian cargo cults,
Japanese new religions, and other groups, there is a
slant that leaves the impression that persons join or
create fringe groups merely to "escape" overwhelming
noxious forces, that they are buffeted helplessly by
larger social changes until they happen on an island
of refuge that gives them religious solace and hope. Analyzing the black Holiness-Pentecostal experience in
American society, Washington (1972:81) succinctly rejected this assumption:

The black ruralites moving to the urban South
and North who joined the permanent sects did
so for the same reason as the majority members
of sects who were urbanites. They did not wan-
der helplessly into them, seeking an intimate
fellowship or primary-group experience, so
much as they came determined to establish a
new set of attitudes and values in an atmos-
phere of certainty. Joining a sect was an in-
tentional act, not an accidental one. (Emphasis mine.)

CASE STUDIES

The two articles selected for discussion below are
not really "classics" in the field. Rather, they are
studies of separate movements by two well known anthropologists who are quite comfortable working within the
revitalization theory perspective. I have chosen them
because they take for granted among the readers the anthropological assumption that such fringe groups function as "bridges" for the social adaptation of their
members.

FIRST CASE

"Religious Conversion as a
Breakthrough for Transculturation:
A Japanese Sect in Hawaii"
Takie Sugiyama Lebra

On a purely theoretical level Lebra (1970) is interested in the logical inevitability of religion's

impact on the secular world and conversely its own adjustment to those secular institutions. Religious faith can provide a believer with a certain autonomy from his social environment, but yet faith must be acted out, and it is here that faith feeds back into the social change process. She observes that converting to an "eccentric sect" (characteristic of "the displaced or lower status strata of a population") yields the first set of circumstances, namely "a systematic completion of alienation from the dominant, respectable strata of society."(183) Yet such conversion can also be a path for ultimate reintegration into larger society. She notes that "conversion to a deviant religion can facilitate the individual's ability to shed his deviant tendency and to readjust himself to the dominant part of society." (183)

Lebra studied the conversions of Japanese immigrants in Hawaii to a millennial sect called Tensho-kotai-jingu-kyo (or Tensho). Tensho, founded in Japan immediately after World War II by a farmer's wife who claimed to "carry God in her abdomen," was popularly known as the Dancing Religion after its practice of members' collective ritualistic dancing in public. Its beliefs were shamanistic and oriented towards healing. Tensho maintained that spirit resides everywhere, with a pantheon of lesser supernatural entities (ghosts, etc.) under the control of a supreme omnipotent deity, the Kami. At some unspecified date in the future a divine trial would be held by Kami, and believers in Tensho would naturally receive favorable verdicts for their souls. Lebra collected interview data from fifty-five first and second generation immigrant Japanese males (out of a total Hawaiian membership of about 500). They were composed disportionately of unskilled menial workers (such as janitors, domestic help, and "irregular"

workers) who had been caught in a vicious circle" of
blocked upward social mobility, negative self-concepts
and feelings of defeatism, extreme sensitivity to ridicule, social isolation, resentment of their better-off
more Americanized fellow Japanese, and a marked resist-
ance to acculturation (i.e., integration into American
culture). Her study is somewhat exceptional in that she
took the trouble to obtain this detailed information.

Tensho encouraged converts to perceive all aspects
of their world, from minor things like headaches to major events like obtaining a better job, as divinely influenced. Every gratifying or pleasant experience, Lebra
says,

> was understood as a sign of the Kami's special
> favor or reward, or of the attainment of sal-
> vation. Conversely, every undesirable experi-
> ence such as physical incapacitation was at-
> tributed either to the Kami's disciplinarian
> punishment or to a certain disposition (hos-
> tility or dependency) of a lesser spirit pos-
> sessing the person. (186)

In this way converts began to be desensitized to
former sources of social sanctions and previous frames
of reference for interpreting their behaviors. This process was accelerated when they were required to participate in the monthly public dancing ritual. The latter
usually shocked outsiders and had a "bridge-burning"
effect on converts. Having comported themselves in so
undignified a manner, they then felt free from the traditional Japanese restraints of shame and "face" and
could make actual breaks if need be with families and
friends.

Members were encouraged to proselytize and were
constantly reminded of the various influential, prestig-
ious individuals who had joined the worldwide movement.

A positive self-image in each member was promoted by lectures and testimonies of role-model members who used their new found "freedom" to be more assertive in finding jobs, managing their lives, and so forth. As representatives of Tensho, members in their regular proselytization activities were exhorted to upgrade their demeanors and personal appearances.

Tensho had a love-hate ambivalence toward worldly success. Capitalizing on the converts' resentment of other Japanese immigrants who went on to find material success, Tensho leaders encouraged members to regard the "maggot" world as transitory and soon to end. "Failure was taken as an asset, whose success was considered to handicap the person, in terms of accessibility to the millenium." (190) Failure became success and vice-versa. Moreover, one's worldly lot was translated into divine will, and the convert was believed to be working out the Kami's predestined strategy for him, however much he suffered in the immediate world, with heaven as an eventual reward. At the same time, Tensho also preached that any successes enjoyed by the convert in this life were rewards by the Kami for the former's devotion. Secular success became interpreted, in a fashion akin to Calvinists of the Protestant Reformation, as a sign of the Kami's favor. Indeed, like Calvinism, not only was worldly success regarded by Tensho members as evidence of spiritual merit, but also members were encouraged by the group to live a sober, disciplined, frugal lifestyle which was highly conducive to relative success. At some point some members even began hiring other members in their businesses, and the sense of success spread.

Lebra interprets the Tensho sect as providing some first and second generation Japanese immigrants with a revitalized religious faith that more directly addressd their social situations. It provided relief for

their interwoven dilemma of low social skills/low social
opportunity/low motivation and optimism. It placed a
new time frame on the duration of their current troubles.
Further, Tensho enabled some to enjoy real social mobility, others at least to feel some relative success, and
still others to at least interpret their low status in
a new hopeful cosmological scheme. Though Lebra does
not use the word, she clearly implies that Tensho func-
tioned as a bridge for these immigrants to acculturate
and better adapt to their new situation. Equipped with
a revitalized faith, many had their lives--from their
own perspectives--improved.

The question which Lebra can of course not answer
without first obtaining longitudinal data on the converts over a lifetime is if Tensho was merely a short-
run haven for persons having difficulty acculturating
but who went on to adjust successfully to larger American society and then found membership in a "weird sect"
a handicap to further mobility. If sect members did not
experience fairly long-range upward mobility, and probably most would not, then the limited "success stories"
found in the movement would provide realistic moderate
goals but not the sort to push the average member into
a success bracket that left him little in common with
other members. In this regard Tensho could survive indefinitely or even go on to expand and stabilize. One
wonders in that case if the "bridge" analogy is an appropriate one, since many who step on never step off.

SECOND CASE

"Leadership and Organization
in the Olive Tree Movement"
Felix Moos

This study, like Moos' similar companion piece
(1964) , offers a basic description of Park Chang No
Kyo, or the Olive Tree Movement (named for the twin al-
legorical Olive Trees of Truth in Revelations 11:4) which
was a Korean new religion founded in the 1950s. The
movement's central figure, Tae Sun Park, was both shaman
and self-proclaimed messiah come to fulfill Isaiah's
prophecy, "Who stirred up one from the East whom victory
meets at every step?" (Isaiah 41:2) Like his Korean new
religions rival, Sun Myung Moon, Park had a Presbyterian
background and spent his young manhood in wartime Japan
obtaining a technical education. However, Park's fortunes multiplied somewhat faster than Moon's. By 1964
Moon had only about 32,000 followers (Syn-duk, 1967),
whereas Park had accumulated somewhere between 1,800,000
and 2,000,000 followers.

After the war Park began his career as an evangelist preacher with a heavy emphasis on healing. In 1955,
for example, Park was a featured speaker at a ten-day
revival sponsored by the Korean Revival Association and
attended by 20,000 persons. Here he began practicing
his faith healing techniques of "Anch'al" (touch of
peace) that aroused a great deal of controversy. Followers believed that Park could transmit divine power
to afflicted individuals through a "vigorous message."
The logical extension soon developed that his mere touch
was efficacious:

Water with which Park washed his feet came
to be a cure-all which would lead whoever drank
it to "eternal life". It was during this initial period of the movement that Park's followers started to call him "Olive Tree," Spiritual "Mother," and the "Righteous Man of the
East." (22)

As his reputation spread, Park became progressively
discontented with the Presbyterian leadership. The feeling was mutual. In 1956 the Presbyterian Church expelled
Park as a heretic. In 1959 he received a two and one-
half-year prison sentence for defrauding and injuring
followers during the Anch'al rite. (He was subsequently
pardoned.) He was jailed several more times on charges
of "tampering" with political elections through influencing his followers' votes, tax evasion, sexual promiscuity, draft evasion, and other accusations clearly in-
dicating that a number of persons, including the politi-
cal-religious establishment, considered him a public
nuisance. Despite what his followers interpreted as persecution, however, Park survived and the movement spread
and financially thrived.

Most of Moos' analysis concerns itself with the
history of the Olive Tree movement and Park's brief bio-
graphy, information on the Zion Educational Foundation
(the name of Park's multifaceted business empire, staff-
ed almost exclusively by followers who work for substan-
tially less than the going wage), the several "Christian
Town" industrial complex communities which made Park
a millionaire and the socio-cultural conditions in which
the movement arose. The last emphasis is particularly
instructive for our purposes here. Moos explicitly views
the Olive Tree movement as a classic revitalization
movement, one of a number of "deliberate, organized and
conscious efforts to integrate traditional patterns with

the plethora of outside influences unleashed by sudden socio-economic change in a given situation of a given society." (27) Until the Japanese surrender in 1945, Korean religious freedom had been severely restricted for 36 years of foreign occupation. The end of war brought the sudden removal of these restrictions as well as enormous uncertainty, social upheaval, and the persistent threat of civil war. These are the standard elements in revitalization theory's model of the conditions producing such movements. These groups typically are led by charismatic, often immodest individuals claiming direct lines of communication and inspiration with the supernatural and possess syncretistic doctrines that mix Confucian, shamanist, Taoist, or whatever indigenous and western Judeo-Christian beliefs. They cast a wide net theologically and function as beacons of optimism that have wide reception among those persons psychologically insecure and economically marginal. Their millennial themes, exemplified by Park's patently obvious references to himself as the fulfillment of Old Testament prophecy and his promise of paradise for true believers, directly reflect their deprivations and aspirations. In a succinct example of the revitalization model approach, complete with reference to the presumed psychological states of converts, Moos writes:

> These new religious cults in Korea have not only helped to fill the psychological vacuum resulting from the end of the Japanese occupation and the subsequent liberation of Korea in 1945 but also have succeeded in providing a seemingly hopeful and more secure psychoeconomic future to many hitherto economically depressed and hopeless individuals. (16)

Unlike Lebra in her study of Tensho, Moos provides little or no evidence for assertions such as the quote

above. The "deprivation assumption" in his revitalization explanation, therefore, remains more tenuous than
he presents it. Moreover, since deprivation on the part
of converts is obviously so intrinsic a part of this
perspective, it might have been worth both authors' respective efforts to explain the presumably nondeprived
who joined. Lebra alludes to such persons, and certainly
not everyone who enlisted in Park's movement would have
been from the lowest social strata. One wonders how
many persons joined either movement out of erotic attraction for a member, or because they had special training or skills which made them exceptionally valuable
for recruitment, or because of subtle pressures from
bosses, mistresses, mates, or neighbors.

   More importantly, unless one wishes to posit that
South Korea is in a perpetual state of widespread turmoil (which it may be politically, but certainly not
on a day-to-day basis for the average person on the
street, at least since the later 1950s) what can a study
like Moos' tell us about the dynamics of the survival
of Park's movement, or for that matter Sun Myung Moon's
(which went on to spread throughout Japan, Europe and
the United States)? Clearly the two questions--HOW DID
IT START? and HOW DOES IT CONTINUE?--are not of the same
level, a fact that does not make the anthropological
revitalization perspective less viable but which does
point out its limitations.

REFERENCES

Barrett, Leonard E. 1977. The Rastafarians. Boston:
    Beacon Press.

_____. 1974. Soul-Force: African Heritage

in Afro-American Religion. Garden City, NY: Doubleday Anchor.

Bromley, David G. and Anson D. Shupe, Jr. 1979. "Moonies" in America: Cult, Church and Crusade. Beverly Hills, CA: Sage.

Burridge, Kenelm. 1969. New Heaven, New Earth: A Study of Millenarian Activities. New York: Schocken Books.

Eister, Allan W. 1974. "Culture Crises and New Religious Movements: A Paradigmatic Statement of a Theory of Cults." Pp. 612-27 in Irving I. Zaretsky and Mark P. Leone, eds., Religious Movements in Contemporary America. Princeton, NJ: Princeton University Press.

Foss, D.A. and R.W. Larkin. 1979. "The Roar of the Lemming: Youth, Postmovement Groups, and the Life Construction Crisis." Pp. 264-85 in Harry M. Johnson, ed., Religious Change and Continuity. San Francisco: Josey Bass.

Geertz, Clifford. 1966. "Religion as a Cultural System." Pp. 1-46 in Michael Banton, ed., Anthropological Approaches to the Study of Religion. London: Tavistock Publications.

_____. 1958. "Ethos, World-View and the Analysis of Sacred Symbols." Antioch Review Winter (1957-58): 421-37.

Ikado, Fujio. 1968. "Trends and Problems of New Religions: Religion in Urban Society." Pp. 101-17 in Kiyomi Morioka and William H. Newell, eds., The Sociology of Japanese Religion. Leiden: E.J. Brill.

La Barre, Weston. 1972. The Ghost Dance. New York: Dell.

Lanternari, Vittorio. 1963. The Religions of the Oppressed. New York: New American Library.

Lebra, Takie Sugiyama. 1970. "Religious Conversion as a Breakthrough for Transculturation: A Japanese

Sect in Hawaii." Journal for the Scientific Study of Religion 9 (Fall): 181-94.

McFarland, H. Neill. 1967. The Rush Hour of the Gods. New York: MacMillan.

Marwick, Max. 1970. "Witchcraft as a Social Strain-Gauge." Pp. 280-95 in Max Marwick, ed., Witchcraft and Sorcery. Baltimore, MD: Penguin Books.

Mooney, James. 1965. The Ghost-Dance Religion and the Sioux Outbreak of 1890. (Originally published in 1896) Chicago: University of Chicago Press.

Moos, Felix. 1967. "Leadership and Organization in the Olive Tree Movement." The New Religions of Korea (Royal Asiatic Society, Transactions of the Korea Branch) 43:11-27.

_____. 1964. "Some Aspects of Park Chang No Kyo--A Korean Revitalization Movement." Antropological Quarterly (July):110-20.

Norbeck, Edward. 1970. Religion and Society in Modern Japan: Continuity and Change. Houston: Tourmaline Press.

Spiro, Melford E. 1966. "Religion: Problems of Definition and Explanation." Pp. 85-126 in Michael Banton ed., Anthropological Approaches to the Study of Religion. London: Travistock Publications.

Syn-duk, Ch'oi. 1967. "Korea's Tong-il Movement." The New Religions of Korea. (Royal Asiatic Society, Transactions of the Korea Branch) 43:167-80.

Thomsen, Harry. 1963. The New Religions of Japan. Rutland, VT: Charles E. Tuttle Company.

Tiryakian, Edward A. 1972. "Toward the Sociology of Eso-teric Culture." American Journal of Sociology 78 (November):491-512.

Wallace, Anthony F.C. 1966. Religion: An Anthropological View. New York: Random House.

_____. 1956. "Revitalization Movements." American Anthropological 58:264-81.

Washington, Jr., Joseph R. 1973. Black Sects and Cults. Garden City, NY: Doubleday Anchor.

Weber, Max. 1964a. The Theory of Social and Economic Organization. Trans. by A.M. Henderson and Talcott Parsons. New York: The Free Press.

_____. 1964b. The Sociology of Religion. Trans. by Ephraim Fischoff. Boston: Beacon Press.

White, Jr., Lynn. 1964. Medieval Technology and Social Change. New York: Oxford University Press.

Williams, F.E., 1934. "The Vailala Madness in Retrospect." Pp. 369-79 in E.E. Evans-Pritchard, Raymond Firth, Bronislaw Malinowski, and Isaac Schapera, eds., Essays Presented to C.G. Seligman. London: Kegan Paul, Trench, Trubner & Co.

Worsley, Peter. 1957. The Trumpet Shall Sound: A Study of Cargo Cults in Melanesia. London: MacGibbon & Kee.

Yinger, J. Milton. 1963. Sociology Looks at Religion. New York: MacMillan.

FURTHER SUGGESTED READING

Bastien, Joseph. 1978. Mountain of the Condor: Metaphor and Ritual in an Andean Avllu. Monograph #64, American Ethnological Society. St. Paul: West Publishing Company.

Brannen, Noah S. 1968. Soka Gakkai, Japan's Militant Buddhists. Richmond, VA: John Knox Press.

Cochrane, Glynn. 1970. Big Men and Cargo Cults. Oxford: Clarendon Press.

Firth, Raymond. 1955. "A Theory of Cargo Cults." Man 142:130-32.

Lincoln, C. Eric. 1961. The Black Muslims in America. Boston: Beacon Press.

Linton, Ralph. 1943. "Nativistic Movements." American
     Anthropologist 45:230-40.

Marwick, Max. 1970. Witchcraft and Sorcery. Baltimore,
     MD: Penguin Books.

May, L. Carlyle. 1954. "The Dancing Religion: A Japanese
     Messianic Sect." Southwestern Journal of Anthro-
     pology 10 (Spring):119-37.

Moody, Edward J. 1974. "Magic Therapy: An Anthropolog-
     ical Investigation of Contemporary Satanism."
     Pp. 355-82 in Irving I. Zaretsky and Mark P. Leone,
     eds., Religious Movements in Contemporary America.
     Princeton, NJ: Princeton University Press.

Opler, Marvin K. 1950. "Two Japanese Religious Sects."
     Southwestern Journal of Anthropology 6 (Spring):
     69-78.

Schwartz, Theodore. 1971. "The Noise: Cargo-Cult Frenzy
     in the South Seas." Psychology Today 4 (March):
     51-4, 102-3.

THOUGHTS FOR FURTHER CONSIDERATION

Imagine that you are a Roman anthropologist in the
first century A.D. Field workers in Palestine report
to your institute about a persistent revitalization
movement, a Jewish messianic cult that not long ago nomadically covered much ground in the area but which almost came to an end in Jerusalem. Its leader was crucified for sedition; his followers scattered throughout
the Middle East to recruit members. The group has no
clear leadership or hierarchy of authority (currently
members seem split into two factions: one group follows
a Greek Jew named Paul, the other obeys a Hebrew in
Jerusalem named James). The movement has yet to produce

even written doctrines or scriptures. All that exists
is an oral tradition of miracle stories (which are not
even very original).

What is your professional prognosis? Given the
group's obvious dependence on socio-political turmoil
for its appeal, how long can it last? What can you assume about the psychological states of the people who
join? Who would have nothing to lose by joining such
a group? What are its odds of survival?

THE SOCIAL PSYCHOLOGICAL
PERSPECTIVE

The social psychological perspective of fringe religions, like social psychology in general, infers the states of mind and thought processes of group members from their overt actions. No one can directly "see" a conversion, for example, but we assume that it has taken place if certain outward behaviors change. These may be straightforward expressions of faith and testimonies, visible adoption of new habits (such as abstinence from sex/drugs/alcohol/tobacco or donning saffron robes in place of western clothes) and new values (such as vegetarianism or pacificism), a new vocabulary and set of topics of conversation (new concern for karma, enlightenment, or salvation) and may or may not include radical readjustments in lifestyle and associates. Converts might be encouraged to drop out of conventional society, as in the case of many communal groups, or conversely, encouraged to become more involved in society's institutions, as we saw in the previous chapter's case analysis of the Tensho sect in Hawaii. In any event, such changes in activities are assumed by this perspective to reflect new attitudes and a new social reality in the mind of the convert.

The general social psychological perspective takes in a broad range of separate theoretical viewpoints. It may be most useful here to conceptualize this perspective's interest in fringe religions as centering around three major issues: "conversion", "faith maintenance", and "defections". These issues address three questions, respectively: WHY DO THEY JOIN? WHY DO THEY STAY? WHY DO THEY LEAVE? Each of these three issues has had several distinctly different sets of answers to the question it asks. One group of researchers looks at the deprivations people suffer as explaining their motivations to join, remain, or cut off membership. Another sees deprivations as important but not sufficient to answer adequately the three questions above. This interactionist group of researchers also maintains that social factors in the fringe group's situation play a determing role in who joins, stays, or leaves. Still other researchers see the answers to these questions in the organizational roles provided by fringe religions, i.e., how and whom do these fringe groups recruit, how do they generate conformity, and why do they fail to hold some members' commitment? A final, fourth group of researchers answers all three questions using a brainwashing model: followers are deceived and hypnotized into joining, kept subservient with "mind control" practices, and only leave when forcibly removed and deprogrammed.

In recent years the issues addressed by the social psychological perspective have attracted a good deal of popular attention and have been the often emotional subjects of discussion by social scientists, scholars of religion, clergymen, lawyers, fringe group members' families, and even physicians. As we shall see, the variations within the social psychological perspective are sometimes sharply in disagreement and represent quite distinct social realities.

THE DEPRIVATION MODEL

Analyses of fringe religious activity which rely on assumptions of deprivation have unquestionably been the most popular with scholars of various disciplines.

Certainly the expectation that prospective converts are predisposed by various social, economic, and psychological (pathological) problems to seek refuge in religious cults and movements has been a mainstay in much of the literature on conversion. For example, in his generally unsympathetic account of fringe religions half a century ago, Binder (1933:192) voiced a popular common sense view about converts:

> One of the most amazing things that arrests our attention is the fact that the cults number among their constituency so many apparently intelligent and otherwise progressive spirits. It is more than likely, however, that not infrequently even the reputed enlightenment of these adherents is offset by some peculiar psychological deficiency or emotional complex.

The source of such deprivations varies according to both the professional orientations of observers and the specific groups in question. Conversion may be attributed to purely psychiatric problems, to social conditions that cause new stresses and strains for particular types of people, or some combination of the two, i.e., where social conditions exacerbate existing latent personal problems. The purely psychiatric position sees the dynamics of personality formation and unconscious conflict worked out in cultic beliefs and practices. Casey (1941), for example, understands participation in the sexual rites of the black mass as a direct explosive revolt against a tyrannical superego, i.e., toward God and the moral authority of conventional society, and simultaneously the resolution of unconscious sexual conflict. Galanter et al. (1979) conclude the conversion to Sun Myung Moon's ascetic Unification Church resulted in a reduction of neurotic stress for some young adult members (though pathology was not found rampant in their sample). Similarly, Moody (1974) notes that feelings of sexual inadequacy and personal powerlessness can be overcome for some members by certain sexual rites in contemporary Satanism that act as progressive desensitization therapy. Anthony and Robbins (1974) claim that conversion to the Meher Baba faith had the effect of reducing alienation in young adult members who previously rejected both the conventional middle-class work ethic and the drug milieu of the 1960s counter-culture. Garrison (1974) likewise concludes from her study of Puerto Rican Pentecostals in a low income New York City neighborhood that sectarian fundamentalism can aid not only in hastening acculturation but also in helping to reduce the stress involved.

Others, such as Moos (1967), discussed as a case study in the previous chapter, view rapid socio-cultural changes as creating psychologically stressful conditions of social disorganization and a breakdown in confidence in traditional religion. Thus, La Barre (1972:197) accounts for human beings' willingness to adopt new revitalized religious forms (in his terminology, "crisis cults") as the product of an interaction between institution-shattering social change and "a biological experience of extended early security that is inveterately sought again when later adaptions go awry." Sociologists (e.g., Glock and Stark, 1965; Glock, 1964) have more broadly defined deprivations to include physical, ethical, and social status deficiencies. These, however, produce the same general consequence of feelings of relative deprivation and subjective stress that presumably motivate persons to investigate alternative religions. Why certain individuals seek a religious solution to their problems rather than engage in political radicalism or turn into alcoholics is, of course, a biographical and psychological matter, which the interactionist approach takes up.

Studies employing the assumption of deprivation invariably limit their attention to the issue of conversion. Once conversion has taken place, it is assumed that the ongoing exchanges between member and fringe group organization are mutually satisfying and for an indefinite time at least provide whatever was missing in the person's life. If he was low in social status and possessed a negative sense of self-worth, the group gives him titles, purpose, and a new elevated in-group status. If he was lonely, the group loves him. If he was unattractive, the group redefines him as beautiful. The other questions of faith maintenance and defection (or disaffiliation), to my knowledge, are rarely if ever discussed. Logically, if the group should disappear or change its character so that it no longer delivers whatever satisfaction the member was deprived of, then the latter will move on. Thus the particular groups are considered functionally equivalent to one another. The deprived person assumedly joined, not for their particular doctrines or other features, but to resolve his deprivation(s). In some cases, such as Moody's (1974) analysis of the self-conscious sexually repressed young man Billy G., once the Satan-worshipping cult which he joined had given him a new confidence in dealing with women, he might expand beyond the pool of females in his coven and eventually drop out of the group altogether. However, to predict that outcome would assume that Billy G. joined only out of sexual deprivation and that only such motives kept him participating.

The deprivation model is certainly not without its critics, particularly in recent writings on fringe religions. Neal's (1970) review of the conversion literature finds three clusters of typically assumed predisposing motives that have their origins in deprivations:

(1) a desire to escape from an unwanted ego or self by immersion in a social movement, (2) a quest for a sense of community and human warmth, and (3) a pursuit of ultimate meaning about life. Neal concludes that the emphasis on motives and the preoccupation with deprivations may in fact be a subtle "put-down" of fringe groups, i.e., that they can be psychologically reduced to mere gaggles of borderline personalities and psychological losers. Yinger (1946:88) dismisses the deprivation model entirely:

> Scholars generally assume that sects and cults produce more emotionally unstable and mentally ill persons then denominations and churches. Many mentally ill persons indeed are found in sects, but there may be proportionately as many in churches. What appears to be a causal relationship may result only from variations in the self-selection that operates in religious bodies with voluntary membership. Athough socially isolated persons may find fellowship and security in a sect and sect preachers occasionally precipitate a psychosis in persons under severe emotional stress, there is no evidence that sect membership is an indication of poor mental health.

Indeed, there is a growing body of research to suggest that assumptions of deprivations, unless verified empirically, can be misleading, confusing cultural abhorence of the unconventional with scientific analysis and retarding our understanding of fringe religions beyond the rather basic question of WHY DO PERSONS JOIN? (Not all researchers, I might add, simply assume deprivation when they utilize the concept. Garrison [1974] measured it among Pentecostals with sophisticated psychological tests while Anthony and Robbins [1974] conducted in-depth interviews to establish its existence with Maher Baba respondents.) In many cases indications of deprivation do not lead one very far. Bromley and Shupe (1979b) do not find severe deprivations in Unification Church members' own retrospective accounts of their conversions--despite obvious temptations for converts to exaggerate what was wrong with their lives before conversion. Most felt they had left something good or nonproblematic for something better. Seggar and Kuntz (1972) do not find exceptional social, economic, health or psychological deprivations in their study of Mormon converts. Most joined through networks of relatives and friends who made use of these relationships to interest them gradually in Mormonism. Garrison (1974:327) does not uncover pathology in her sample of Puerto Rican Pentecostals:

> If it is deviant to be sectarian and to "speak
> in tongues", then they are deviants. But, if
> we demand some other criteria such as inade-
> quate functioning in occupational or social
> roles, or emotional disturbance, we have found
> no evidence of it.

Likewise, Hine (1974) does not find widespread socio-economic deprivation in her study of Pentecostal converts. Her findings mirror Bromley and Shupe's in that Pentecostals did not join as a way of fleeing some noxious situation. She argues that to speak in terms of predispositional deprivations would be inaccurate:

> Many of our informants reported the fact that
> they were perfectly satisfied with the domin-
> ant standards of society and with their own
> and others' behavior until a committed re-
> cruiter in a position to influence his think-
> ing sensitized him to Biblical standards. In
> these instances perceived behavioral depriva-
> tion is an effect of movement dynamics, not

a precondition, and we would be left explain-

ing a phenomenon in terms of itself. (655)

Nor is evidence of pathological deprivation to be found in the decade-long study of a communal Jesus Movement sect by Richardson, Stewart and Simmonds (1979), a project involving conventional personality inventory instruments, nor in the rigorous psychiatric studies of members of various new religions of the 1970s by Levine and Salter (1976), or Ungerleider and Wellisch (1979a, 1979b). Heirich (1977), investigating Catholic Pentecostal converts and comparing them with a control group, did find signs of stress in the backgrounds of the converts, but he also found just as much stress in the nonconvert group. The concept of deprivation, in other words, did not discriminate joiners from nonjoiners.

Admitting that much of the previous research questioning the limits of deprivational assumptions is recent, what can account for the persistent popularity of this approach? Aside from the Western penchant for psychologizing and psychoanalyzing social behavior and the intellectual laziness which is promoted by simply stereotyping all members of fringe religions as mentally impaired or deprived, there are several other reasons which can be identified.

First and foremost, many people with indisputable problems do seek religious solutions. Religion has never been loathe to remind us of its efficacy in problem solving of all types, from small matters to miracles, and thus if there is a socialized religious viewpoint for problem solving, likely many in our Western societies share it. I am not arguing that deprived people can not and do not find what they lack in religion. (The extent to which they compose part of a majority of any given religion, however, is an empirical matter.) Their real presence in fringe religious groups undoubtedly provides partial reinforcement to those scholars assuming universal deprivations.

Second, the beliefs and practices of many fringe groups are poorly understood, and so their lifestyles are ethnocentrically interpreted. Their social realities are not those of outside observers. Their doctrines may seem ludicrous, incomprehensible, heretical or dangerous, depending on one's point of view, but the observer's unfamiliarity or disagreement with them often lends them a quality of "not being reasonable." The conclusion: only someone crazy could believe something like that.

Third, many fringe groups lack social status. Their members as individuals may be lower class, poorly educated, perhaps of a racial or ethnic minority with a distinct subcultural tradition. Their observers are frequently just the opposite. This third reason dovetails with the second: the Pentecostal speaking in tongues, sweating, weeping, fainting as he works his way through his religious service, worships in a social reality light years away from that of the agnostic or mainline Protestant academic. To the latter these behaviors may simply not look "normal", and thus the hunt begins for their abnormal origins.

THE INTERACTIONIST MODEL

The interactionist approach does not throw out the assumption that deprivations motivate people to join fringe religions. It simply maintains that such motivations alone are not adequate to explain fringe participation since undoubtedly many more persons experience deprivations of one sort or another than ever join such groups. Besides deprivations, social factors of the

fringe group in question, both internal, (members' de-
pendency on one another) and external (its relation with
majority society) require consideration to round out
the picture of conversion, faith maintenance, and defection.

Without question the classic statement of this approach is the article by Lofland and Stark (1965; see
also Lofland, 1966) entitled "Becoming a World-Saver:
A Theory of Conversion to a Deviant Perspective." While
I discuss it more fully as a case study later in this
chapter, it can be summarily described as an examination
of conversion to the early Unification Church in the
United States, giving equal attention and importance
to "predispositional" and "situational" factors. The
former predispositional factors include a broadly defined array of problems or tensions, a previously learned tendency to view the world and personal problems in
religious terms, and a self-definition of oneself as
a religious seeker. The latter situational factors which
arise from contacts between conversion candidates and
fringe religious group members are composed of a "tip-
ping point" where crossroads of decision prompted by
other developments in the person's life are arrived at
and passed, the dual development of affective relations
between convertee and converters and the erosion of similar relations between convertee and former friends,
relatives, etc., and a period of intensive "moving in"
of the convertee with his missionaries that culminates
in what is commonly regarded as conversion.

The Lofland-Stark model has inspired a good deal
of additional research and theorizing on conversion that
either criticizes or extends its logic (e.g., Lynch,
1977; Richardson and Steward, 1977; Seggar and Kuntz,
1972). Lofland himself (1977) has reexamined his interactionist theory and now views it as too "deterministic"

and not giving individuals enough credit for actively seeking their own conversions. However, it was the first major attempt to explain why certain persons translate their problems into religious terms and seek a guru while other persons end up in a psychiatrist's office. The model pays virtually no attention to the issue of defection and disaffiliation except implicitly, i.e., the group may no longer be able to resolve personal tensions, it might cause new ones, or the relative strength of affective bonds inside and outside the group might shift in favor of the decision to pack it all in and leave. Logically one could predict that the elements that go to compose the interactionist model could be withdrawn one by one or rearranged to account for departure in a fashion parallel to entry.

A classic statement of why people do not leave a fringe group in the face of inescapable evidence that discredits its doctrine, thus relevant to issues of faith maintenance and defection, is the Festinger et al. study of a UFO cult entitled When Prophecy Fails (1964). Since their study too is considered in more detail later in this chapter, I simply note here that it examines a particular question of faith maintenance for a special kind of fringe religion--one that makes a clear-cut prophecy for a specific date. In the group researched by Festinger et al. the prophecy (cataclysmic destruction of North America and a rescue-by-flying-saucer of the "elect" believers) repeatedly failed to materialize and yet each fiasco seemingly strengthened, not weakened, the faith of some members. The psychological dynamics of this process constitute the theme of their study. While not directly concerned with tensions or problematic predispositions leading to conversion, the researchers do discuss these in the context of persons' initial motives to found or join the cult. A simi-

lar but less extensive treatment of the faith-mainten-
ance-in-the-face-of-public-rejection problem is Simmons'
(1964) study of a community of deviant believers which
he refers to as Espers. (Interestingly enough, Simmons
held conventional academic positions with the Universities of Illinois and California before becoming a
Scientologist.)

The interactionist model starts from the very common sense assumption of deprivation theorists that people
need to be motivated to seek change either of themselves
or of society. However, its obvious contribution is in
its attempt to distinguish those who take the religious
route to satisfying their wants or resolving their problems from those who do not, and in explaining the mechanisms by which some keep their new-found faith and
others abandon it.

ROLE THEORY

A role theory approach to conversion, faith maintenance, and defection develops from two basic sociological concepts: "status" (a given position in an organization) and "role" (normative behavior appropriate
to a given status). It offers an organizational view
of the process of becoming (and unbecoming) a fringe
religious group member as opposed to the more frequently
encountered psychological view. As such it is less concerned with the motives that initially lead persons to
consider adopting a new faith since many fringe groups
(particularly the communally organized ones) reshape
motives to fit their own organizational needs. (For example, a young man may first become interested in the
Unification Church through a physical or romantic attraction to one of its female witnesses, but he does
not remain in the movement very long before he learns

that all members regard each other as literal brothers and sisters and, to keep harmony within their crowded communal living centers, remain strictly celibate before their arranged marriages.) Role theory conceptualizes conversion, faith maintenance, and defection not as separate states in some natural cycle but rather as ongoing processes. These processes involve sequences of status positions into which persons move and learn the accompanying roles.

As early as 1952 Zetterberg (1952:165) suggested that "the religious conversion proper is a sudden acceptance of a social role advocated by a religious group." However, it was not until the 1970s that a number of separate researchers began spontaneously to employ this view in studying fringe religions. Bromley and Shupe (1979b) found in their field work with a Unification Church evangelistic team that conversion to the "Moonies" was best understood not as an identifiable before-after event but (contrary to popular media accounts of overnight or "snapping" transformations) as an unfolding process of adopting successive roles in the movement, each role entailing progressively greater commitments and lifestyle changes as well as rewards. The critical components of this role sequence were identified as (1) varied individual predisposing factors, (2) attraction to the movement, (3) initial involvement by persons willing to join in movement activities at least tentatively, (4) active involvement as the experimental participation becomes more permanent, and (5) progressively greater degrees of commitment. One significant finding was that predispositions of Unificationist members before joining were found to be multifarious and hardly pathological in the majority of cases --not manifesting extreme alienation or severe unhappiness in their premembership lives. Predispositions in

fact contributed little to an understanding of who joined, as the organization recruited on a nonselective basis (within a certain youthful age range) and then sought
to shift members' original motives toward those more
suitable to the communal movement. Just as important
was the finding that many members did not join out of
an attraction to the group's ideology--some long-term
members displayed a surprisingly minimal knowledge of
its beliefs--but rather because of its communal lifestyle. Since Unification theology is complex, Bromley
and Shupe concluded that the active role of a communal
member, a role which could be learned in a fairly short
period of time and which enabled a member to function
in convincingly outward manner as a "Moonie", was learned prior to any meaningful change in intellectual (belief) orientation. This sequence of acting followed by
attitude change is a familiar one to social psychologists. (See, e.g., Bem, 1967, 1965; Lieberman, 1956.)

Other sociologists have employed role theory in
similar ways. Bainbridge and Stark (1980) view the status of "clear", i.e., the negative psychological influence of past experiences is now removed, within Scientology as one in a hierarchy of organized positions whose
roles function to minimize doubts, disaffections and
challenges to the organization. The "clear" attains this
status through expensive and lengthy "treatment" ses-
sions, possesses only ambiguous criteria for judging
if "clear" has been achieved, and is under enormous
pressure to agree outwardly that the status is worth
the cost and effort. In another study (Stark and Bainbridge, 1980) they note that Mormons have traditionally
relied for much of their conversion success on friends
and relatives recruiting friends and relatives through
already established intimate role networks. Richardson
(e.g., 1980) in reviewing conversion studies, has even

conceptualized conversion as part of a larger sequence that involves some persons on a lifelong basis. Such persons experience literally "conversion careers", not necessarily "hopping" from fringe group to fringe group randomly but cumulatively building a personal set of beliefs that are continuously modified and added to which lead the persons to explore a variety of beliefs.

In a series of articles concerned with the UFO cult of Bo and Peep, Balch (1980, 1979) and Balch and Taylor (1978, 1977, 1976) have studied how people got in and out in role terms. The member's role involved a taboo on voicing doubts and easily learned overt behaviors that gave other members and outsiders the impression of deep commitment. In fact, the role called for encounters with nonmembers to be deliberately managed in such a way as to give outsiders the impression that the cult had transformed members into glassy-eyed automatons. Members performed their roles so well to each other that defections often seemed abrupt, without any prior signs of dissatisfaction. Balch (1980:142) concluded:

> The private reality of life in a religious cult usually remains hidden behind a public facade of religious fanaticism . . . . The first step in conversion to cults is learning to act like a convert by outwardly conforming to a narrowly prescribed set of role expectations. Genuine conviction develops later beneath a facade of total commitment, and it fluctuates widely during the course of the typical member's career. Many cult members never become true believers, but their questioning may be effectively hidden from everyone but their closest associates.

In sum, role theory approaches the social psychological changes involved in conversion, faith maintenance, and defection from a different set of concepts
than other approaches. A review of recent role theory
literature on fringe religions allows us to conclude
several empirical generalizations about these phenomena.
First, just as falling in love realistically involves
a process of initial progressing into a deepening, more
complex relationship of commitment, so conversion is
best understood as a process (what Bromley and Shupe,
1979b, term the "affiliative process") which may be in-
terrupted or terminated at any time, rather than as a
discrete event. True, there are cases of "love at first
sight" just as there are the on-the-spot decisions to
join a fringe religion. These instances are relatively
rare, however, and not as mysterious as they appear at
first. Likewise, defection may physically occur quickly,
but it too has antecedents and is the result of a gradual process. Following the love analogy, most people do
not "fall out of love", or deconvert, except through
a gradual reinterpretation of their relationships.

Second, many persons join fringe religions for a
variety of motives and regard their membership as experimental and tentative. Membership can be understood
as premised on an exchange equation. As long as the
costs of membership (sacrifices, demands, etc.) do not
exceed the benefits, members will continue to act out
their assigned, expected roles.

Third, a significant point in light of the current
claims about "mind control" and "brainwashing" (see the
following section) is that role theory applications such
as I have briefly reviewed here include an element of
voluntarism in conversion. This is an assumption born
out by sociological research. The active seekership of
many persons seems difficult to refute empirically,

regardless of how bizarre their religious choices may seem. New awareness of this voluntarism in the role theory approach is the result of a general shift of assumptions by some social scientists (see, e.g., Richardson, 1979; Straus, 1978; Lofland, 1977) concerning conversion. In this new perspective persons are not viewed as passive, helpless, perhaps pathological beings upon whom conversion is done but rather as active, conscious seekers pursuing self-actualization and meaning in a pluralistic religious environment.

THE BRAINWASHING MODEL

As I mentioned in "The Criminological Perspective" the idea that fringe religious leaders might possess mysterious powers to attract and manipulate their followers is not new; Father Divine, for example, was credited with such Svengalian abilities over two generations ago. However, it remained for the current wave of new religions making their appearance in the late 1960s and 1970s to inspire a full-blown model of this alleged "mind control". The immediate origins of this model can be traced to the post-World War II cold war and the reports of "brainwashing" of captured American servicemen in Korea as well as to the "thought reform" workshops conducted by communist Chinese.[1] A series of influential postwar articles and books (Hunter, 1962, 1953; Lifton, 1961, 1956; Sargent, 1957; Meerloo, 1956) shocked Americans with the possibilities of psychological conditioning applied under coercive conditions. Films such as The Manchurian Candidate dramatically accentuated the presumably limitless ability of brainwashing agents to breakdown free will and implant new malicious suggestions in the minds of ordinary persons. During the 1970s a new wave of popular books (e.g., Bowart,

1978) accused United States government agencies such
as the Central Intelligence Agency of employing manipulative psychological techniques as standard procedure.

That persons can have their normal free will subverted is of course not an uniquely modern concern. It
has a rich legacy going back to early antiquity in beliefs of demon possession found in virtually every religious tradition.[2] What prompted the "brainwashing"
explanation of new religious participation in the 1970s
was the sudden appearance and/or growth spurts of various fringe groups such as Sun Myung Moon's Unification
Church, the Children of God, the Church of Scientology,
the Way, Hare Krishna, and the popularity of Transcendental Meditation. In a grass roots anti-movement that
began spontaneously across the United States but which
soon coalesced into regional parents' and clergymen's
groups, families shared their accounts of offspring suddenly abandoning educational and career plans, forsaking
fiancés and stereos, and rejecting their parents' aspirations and values as shallow, materialistic, or even
Satanic. Most parents agreed that following these mysterious conversions their offspring seemed to have
changed personalities. This impression was particularly
distressing since their offsprings' new allegiances to
various fringe religious groups seemed as intense and
disturbingly single-minded as they were abrupt.

Research on the origins of the modern American anti-
cult movement (see Shupe and Bromley, 1980a) reveals
that initially parents and other family members were
at a loss to explain these sudden changes. Nothing in
their offsprings' earlier lives had prepared families
for this sudden rash of altruistic, often ascetic ideal-
ism. The 1960s had been years of experiment and change
for many young adults, but not of passionate utopian
religious commitment. It was not long, however, before

parents, many of whom were college-educated professionals, discovered the existing postwar psychological warfare literature. By 1973 labels like "mind control" and
"brainwashing" were already being used, and the various
fringe religions receiving high exposure in the media
were commonly referred to by the pejorative catchall
label of "cults". Parents interpreted their offsprings'
participation as involuntary and pointed to horrorific
tales told by ex-"cult" members as evidence that young
adults were kept in such groups by authoritarian leaders
that employed physical and psychological coercion. A
number of professional sympathizers, frequently either
psychiatrists and psychologists (see, for example, Clark,
1979; Singer, 1979; Verdier, 1977) or explicitly evangelical Christian social scientists (e.g., Enroth, 1979,
1977; Streiker, 1978) provided this anti-cult movement
with legitimacy by accepting at face value the negative
testimonies of angry exfringe group members and general-
izing their allegations to a vaguely defined set of
groups termed "cults".

Thus proponents of the brainwashing model do not
really regard conversion to fringe religions as actual
conversion. They refer to it as "pseudo-conversion",
maintaining that true conversion requires that a person
consciously and rationally make a decision to change
faiths, fully informed of the various ramifications of
this decision. Decisions to join various fringe religions, they staunchly claim, take place under conditions
of confusion, fear and deliberate manipulation which
fail to meet the criteria of "true" conversions.

Once the young offsprings' conversions and continued participation have been defined as involuntary and
the results of psychological captivity, or what has been
referred to as "programming", the logical antidote is

a reversal of the process, or a "deprogramming". Deprogramming has been at the center of the new religions controversy ever since its inception in the early 1970s. Its advocates (in particular Conway and Siegelman, 1978) claim it is a new valuable tool of mental therapy treating what is actually a new disease (i.e., "cultism") and not simply unpopular conversion. Its critics passionately denounce it as organized religious repression under the guise of medical science, that like the Soviets we are in danger of labelling all dissenters as crazy and then treating them as such. The primary anti-brainwashing model argument is that brainwashing involves the elements of coercion (i.e., incarceration) and fear while most fringe religions' converts go to the initial meetings or lectures voluntarily, are not physically held against their wills, and any fear generated is not out of physical danger but is the same as the spiritual anxiety aroused during any fundamentalist revival. Therefore, they say, accusations of brainwashing are empirically unsound and ethnocentrically and indiscriminately applied to all religious straying from the narrow norm of mainline Judeo-Christian religion. They also attack the supposed efficacy of classical brainwashing examples. They charge that the entire concept of a mysterious brainwashing technique developed by communists has been grossly exaggerated with regard to its success. Scheflin and Opton (1978:89), for example, note that out of approximately 3,500 Americans taken prisoner during the Korean War, only about 50 even made pro-communist anti-American statements and only about 25 POWs refused repatriation when the war ended. These authors conclude:

> These numbers do not add up to a persuasive
> case that the Communists developed a method

to control the mind. . . . In the civil war
. . .about two percent of the Union soldiers
captured by the South enlisted in the Confed-
eration.

In other words, comparing civil war defection rates to
the numbers of allegedly brainwashed American POWs ca-
pitulating to the enemy, the former outweigh the latter
by a ratio of two to one. Proponents of the brainwashing
model would counter that deception in "cult" recruiting
is widespread; that psychological coercion and systematic techniques of generating guilt, confusion, and un-
critical acceptance of doctrines can be as devastating
as physical coercion and terror; and that moreover this
new type of brainwashing is more insidious because it
is protected by law under the mantle of religious freedom.

The refutation of claims, the support of counterarguments and alternative perspectives, and the resolution of the validity or falsity of the brainwashing model would require much more space than is available here.
This issue is undoubtedly one of the most complex and
emotionally volatile in twentieth century North American
religion. From a critical standpoint much of the so-
called evidence for brainwashing is hearsay and ethnocentric misinterpretations that exonerate the families
of "cult" members or save face for a number of idealistic
youth who have to account in some way for having made
a mistake in judgment. Social science models that view
the deprogramming situation as one of reintegration of
the nuclear family unit (see Beckford, 1981, 1978) or
as a raw exercise of power by the family to restore
authority over an errant member (e.g., Bromley,Busching,
and Shupe, 1980; Shupe and Bromley, 1980b) have been
virtually ignored by proponents of the brainwashing model. The outspoken professional supporters of the anti-

cult movement typically fail to consider the existing
body of research (for example, Levine and Salter, 1976;
Ungerleider and Wellisch, 1979a, 1979b) finding no ill
psychiatric effects of membership in fringe religions.
They also ignore the rather obvious difficulties and
distortions involved in attempting to lump together various fringe groups holding disparate beliefs and organizational patterns under the category of "cults". (For
a good critique of this stereotyping, see Robbins and
Anthony, 1979.) While there is at best rather mixed support among scholars for the brainwashing model, however,
there is little question that it has become one of the
most widespread publicly accepted perspectives of fringe
religions in recent times.

A NOTE ON PSYCHOLOGICAL REDUCTIONISM

From the standpoints of members of fringe religions
and of many scholars of religion, all four models discussed in this chapter engage in some form of sociological or psychological reductionism. That is, they attempt
to explain the essence of the phenomena of one domain
by the terms and concepts of another. Thus conversion
is reduced to the acting out of unconscious psychological complexes or feelings of deprivation (sometimes interacting with the network of social relationships in
which the convert is embedded), or is reduced to demands
for behavioral and ideological conformity of the stipu-
lated roles of status positions into which converts enter, or is explained away as the result of hypnotic
techniques of manipulative "cult" leaders who implant
their own designs into the helpless brains of the so-
called converts. In none of the models are the believers
explicitly given credit for actually believing their
new faiths, nor is it assumed as part of any model that

they might pursue new spiritual truth as part of a higher, more aesthetic need which humanistic psychologists term "self-actualization". The role theory model (and this may reveal my own bias) seems the least reductionist because it makes no assumption about how people come to adopt their new religious roles. In fact, most role theory research rejects extreme deprivational assumptions and does quite well without such references to them since initial motives to convert are often poor explanations of why people remain in fringe groups over time. When initial motives are considered, this model's lack of presuppositions about deprivations means that it will find self-actualization motives if these are expressed by members. However, insofar as it explains conversion, faith maintenance and even defection in terms of commitment to structural features of the group rather than by reference to theological issues, it could be considered (from a believer's standpoint) reductionistic.

The brainwashing model is obviously the most baldly reductionistic, for it does not even accord many fringe groups legitimacy as religions. In its view there is no real conversion because the fringe group is not a bonafide religion. There are only mad, enslaving gurus and hapless youthful victims. There is no faith maintenance because fringe group members have no real faith. They are assumed to be mental robots. They do not defect or leave voluntarily because they are believed to be incapable of doing so. The brainwashing model's assumptions are actually identical to those of the exploitive sub-type of the criminological perspective and are only presented here because the model couches its arguments in psychological terminology.

Finally, the deprivation perspective, or some variation on it such as the interactionist model, will probably continue to be popular, no doubt in part because of the common sense reaction to religious deviance which even scholars can be expected to register. Extraordinary groups do not simply attract at random ordinary persons, goes the inevitable line of thinking, and if apparent differences in their social, physical or economic circumstances are not manifest among believers, one can always retreat to the less viable, less understood, and therefore more flexible psychological dimension.

CASE STUDIES

The following pair of case studies represents more than famous research examples. Each presents or demonstrates an important social science theory that has had widespread influence on the social psychological understanding of fringe religions. They do not address the same questions, thus in many ways they are not comparable. Readers are strongly urged to pursue each further, however, beyond my own brief reviews of them.

First Case

When Prophecy Fails
Leon Festinger, Henry W. Riecken
and Stanley Schachter

The Festinger et al. study of a millenarian UFO cult is a gem of ethnographic detail, written in a popular readable style that almost causes the reader to forget its primary purpose: to demonstrate the social psychological theory of attitude change which Festinger

developed, called the theory of cognitive dissonance.
Briefly, cognitive dissonance deals with what presumably
occurs in a person's consciousness when he becomes aware
of two inconsistent (dissonant) cognitions or thoughts
about himself, his behavior, the world, or whatever.
This dissonance causes stress, and if stressful enough
the person will try to eliminate it. Dissonance can be
reduced or wiped away by several strategies: ignore the
inconsistent cognitions, obtain new information that
resolves the apparent dissonance, or adjust one of the
cognitions to be more compatible with the other. Thus,
if a woman is taking an oral contraceptive and she reads
in a magazine that a French doctor has conclusively
proved that the pill quadruples the chances of a woman
contracting cancer of the cervix, she can have two dissonant cognitions ("I take the pill, and the pill has
been proven harmful.") and can reduce the dissonance
by one of several actions:

1. Stop reading such articles and not think about
the matter further.
2. Stop taking the pill.
3. Either obtain information that would qualify
the cognition about the doctor's research (for instance that it only applies to European women or
that the research was really conducted on labora-
tory mice) or rationalize away the dissonance (e.g.,
admit the risk but accept it in exchange for freedom from the worry of pregnancy).

What is important in the woman's three possible resolu-
tions of dissonance is that action one really doesn't
resolve it; also action one only ignores the dissonance
(but does resolve the problem caused by it); action two
involves a change of her behavior, but may be costly
or inconvenient to her; in action three either way involves a change of the cognitions about the research.

The cognition about her behavior (taking the pill) may be important enough for her not to change it but rather to alter the other, more malleable cognition.

Cognitive dissonance theory maintains that in such situations of dissonance, reduction cognitions about one's own actions are more resistant to change, particularly if the action has a "bridge-burning" quality to it. This is precisely the case with the type of millenarian movement which Festinger et al. studied. As they put the dilemma:

> Suppose an individual believes something with his whole heart; suppose further that he has a commitment to this belief, that he has taken irrevocable actions because of it; finally suppose that he is presented with evidence, unequivocal and undeniable evidence, that his belief is wrong; what will happen? The individual will frequently emerge, not only unshaken, but even more convinced of the truth of his beliefs than ever before. Indeed, he may even show a new fervor about convincing and converting other people to his view. (3)

This seems the reverse of common sense, but that sort of perverse hypothesizing is typical of cognitive dissonance theory. In such situations the human mind acts according to a logic, but it is not our familiar conscious logic; rather, it is more unconscious, self-serving, defensive. People will change the cognition least resistant to amendment, and knowledge of specific acts are not easily amended or denied. Better to patch up the beliefs in whose name the action was performed. Thus, according to cognitive dissonance theory, Festinger et al. would expect an increase in religious fervor and belief after an irrefutable disconfirmation of prophecy when five conditions are met:

1.   The belief is held with great conviction and is relevant to specific actions of the believer.

2.   The believer must have clearly committed himself in such a way that he has "burned his bridges" behind him and cannot easily return to his nonbelieving past.

3.   The belief or prophecy must be specific about prophesized events in the empirical world.

4.   Disconfirming evidence must happen and be recognized as having happened by that person.

5.   The believer who has gone through this sequence of belief/expectation/disconfirmation must receive social support from like-minded (like-disappointed) believers.

Festinger et al. studied a UFO cult which began in the north central United States. The founder, a housewife who had dabbled previously in Theosophy, the I AM movement, Dianetics (the early form of Scientology) and spiritualism, among other fringe beliefs, had suddenly been awakened one night by a strange sensation in her arm. Seizing pencil and paper, aliens allegedly began communicating with her, initially through the spirit of her dead father, by "automatic writing" that allowed her hand to transcribe their message without her conscious effort. These extraterrestrials inhabited the planets Clarion and Cerus and eventually revealed to her and the small circle of believers she assembled (most of whom had had occult experiences before) that the earth would soon be visited by a terrible disaster: the Great Lakes would flood the interior of the United States, the Atlantic seaboard would submerge, a new mountain range would be thrown up in the central states, and not only would Egypt's deserts be made fertile but also the continent of Mu would rise in the Pacific, among other alterations.

To sum up briefly the chain of events: specific dates and repeated predictions of saucer arrivals to scoop up the faithful remnant shortly before the disaster came and went without the slightest confirmation. At first the transparent rationalizations of members were fairly easily and mutually swallowed: believers could accept postponements and repress their disappointments. As the group attracted publicity and "bridges had to be burned", however, pressures to remain or defect grew. Members quit jobs (or were fired) and broke off relations with their anxious families. The night of the group's first expected saucer visitation their all night vigil in one member's backyard was a fiasco. A second expectation also fell flat as well as other minor ones. Finally, the believers divided into two groups: those who persisted in believing in the UFO message, and those who abandoned it.

What distinguished them--and this determines the reaction to disconfirmed prophecy--was their amount of social support at the time of disconfirmation. That is, were they embedded in supportive circumstances of like-minded believers who helped reach a plausible, acceptable revision of the prophecy, or were they alone when they confronted the fact that the prophecy had failed? The former believers retained their faith (though not without some effort); the latter invariably abandoned it.

This particular application of cognitive dissonance theory is important for the study of fringe religions since so many groups are obsessed by millenarian expectations. Seventh-Day Adventists, Jehovah's Witnesses, the Children of God, and Sun Myung Moon's Unification Church are merely a few of the recent groups expecting great events to occur imminently. As in the group of Festinger et al.'s study, there is no reason to think they cannot explain unfulfilled prophecy to their members without thinning their ranks. That religious belief does not depend solely on the logical consequences of prophecy and real world experience is well illustrated by Festinger et al. It is not unfulfilled prophecy per se that irrevocably disillusions believers, but rather it is the social conditions in which such disconfirmations are received that determine their ultimate impact on faith.[3]

Second Case

"Becoming a World-Saver:
A Theory of Conversion
to a Deviant Perspective"
John Lofland and Rodney Stark

One colleague of mine referred to the Lofland-Stark interactionist model of conversion as the most widely cited conversion model in the literature of sociology. While I suspect that many sociologists would, if asked, place their viewpoints closer to the deprivation model, undoubtedly my colleague is correct in terms of conversion research. Until sociologists recently began utilizing role theory in reconceptualizing what occurs during the process of conversion, Lofland-Stark's has been the predominant sociological model of the phenomenon.

The model is composed of two classes of factors: "predisposing conditions" and "situational contingencies." The former are individuals' attributes prior to conversion. The latter are the immediate conditions involving confrontation and interactions between potential converts and fringe group members.

The predisposing conditions involve three elements:

1. Feelings of tension or deprivation (as defined by the convert himself/herself) of some duration.

2. A uniquely religious perspective for problem solving (and not a political or psychiatric perspective which of course would lead some persons to consider more secular solutions).

3. A perception of oneself as a "seeker" after religious truth.

There are four significant situational factors:

1. A "turning point" or sudden opportunity to change the course of one's life, abandon old patterns, and choose new options is reached when former lifestyles, etc. cease to be relevant.

2. The cultivation or intensification of emotional bonds between potential converts and fringe group members occurs.

3. Relations of the potential convert with non-fringe members atrophy and come to play less and less importance in the former's life so that he feels free to make a verbal conversion.

4. Exclusive, communal interaction with the fringe members intensifies (usually when the convert physicallly moves in with them) and a total or behavioral conversion is complete.

In other words, tensions or deprivations are fine for discussing the initial motives that impel people to act to change their situation; religious problem solving world views and self-definitions of persons as seekers are also important to account for why some persons steer toward innovative religious groups. But not all such persons join up, and it is the second class of interactive factors which this model employs to distinguish the joiners from the nonjoiners. Persons must have reached some crisis point or come to where they are ready to be free from the dysfunctional rut in which they find themselves. Their relations with members of the fringe groups are critical: if they begin to maximize their contacts solely with the fringe group's members and minimize contacts with nonmembers, they are on the way to a verbal conversion. Total conversion is achieved by the convert actually moving in with the fringe group. This move has the function of severing virtually all nongroup contacts and responsibilities of any importance and leaves the convert encapsulated in an emotionally intense, reinforcing environment.

This is the interactionist model developed out of Lofland and Stark's two-year field observation of a tiny millenarian Korean cult in the San Francisco Bay area during the early 1960s. The model has received a good deal of additional attention in recent years because this deviant cult was the first important American missionary foothold of what was to grow into the Unification Church of America. The pseudonyms which Lofland and Stark use to disguise the Church's main personages and doctrines (e.g., Mr. Chang for Rev. Moon, the Divine Precepts for the movement's main scripture, the Divine Principle) now seem amusingly obvious, and despite Lofland's continued refusal to compromise his original assurance of complete anonymity to those early respondents, there is no longer any doubt that the insignificant fringe group he and Stark studied in the early 1960s eventually "made good" in the 1970s.

The model has come under some criticism of late, mainly because of its inclusion of deprivations as a necessary ingredient in conversion. A number of researchers mentioned earlier in this chapter have simply not found the deprivational element of much use or even validity. Lofland (1977) himself has criticized the model for giving the impression that converts are, in reductionistic fashion, passive victims of their own personal problems and of the forces of group dynamics. Others (e.g., Bromley and Shupe, 1979b) have found tensions such as alienation from society more an aftereffect or product of participating in a socially deviant group than a precondition of converts. Stark's own more recent conversion research (see Stark and Bainbridge, 1980) has shifted almost exclusively to considering interactional networks and how they account for conversion.

At the same time it is well to remember that no scientific model of any phenomenon stands forever. Indeed, scientific understanding only progresses by usurping and replacing older models that once served their purpose to stimulate thinking and research with newer, more relevant paradigms. The Lofland-Stark model has generated a good deal of research exploring the limitations of its assertions, and in the process the social psychological conceptualization of conversion has been advanced. We now know that the conversion experience, however personal and intimate for the individual, is inextricably bound up on the patterned processes of social interaction. Sociologically speaking, conversion can no longer be understood as simply acting out personal problems in religious terms; rather, Lofland and Stark restored to conversion the basic social significance which emerges from the interaction within a religious community.

NOTES

[1] The term "brainwashing" is actually a vulgarization for the Chinese characters meaning "to cleanse thoughts", i.e., to achieve ideological (Marxist) purity from the communist's point of view. The term "thought reform" probably better corresponds to the original meaning of the Chinese than does "brainwashing". The latter metaphor possesses a certain bluntness and ruthlessness about it, however, that no doubt explains its continued use.

[2] Explicit parallels between medieval European assumptions of exorcism and twentieth century deprogramming can be found developed in Shupe and Bromley (1980a) and Shupe, Spielmann, and Stigall (1977).

[3] Melton (1980) has examined the Seventh-Day Adventist Church and other millennial movements and concluded that findings from the Festinger et al. study have been overgeneralized and show a simplistic understanding of the role of prophecy in emerging religious movements. While there is not space here to present Melton's counterarguments, it is well to note that the Festinger et al. study is not without its critics.

REFERENCES

Allison, Joel. 1973. "Adaptive Regression and Intensive Religious Experiences." Pp. 308-38 in Benjamin Beit-Hallahmi, ed., <u>Research</u> <u>in</u> <u>Religious</u> <u>Behavior</u>. Monterey, CA: Brooks-Cole.

Anthony, Dick and Thomas Robbins. 1974. "The Meher Baba Movement: Its Affect on Post-Adolescent Social Alienation." Pp. 479-511 in Irving I. Zaretsky and Mark P. Leone, eds., <u>Relgious</u> <u>Movements</u> <u>in</u>

Contemporary America. Princeton, NJ: Princeton Uni-
     versity Press.
Bainbridge, William Sims and Rodney Stark. 1980. "Scien-
     tology: To Be Perfectly Clear." Sociological Analy-
     sis 41 (Summer): 128-36.
Balch, Robert. 1979. "Two Models of Conversion and Com-
     mitment in a UFO Cult." Paper presented at the
     annual meeting of the Pacific Sociological Associa-
     tion. Anaheim, CA.
_____. 1980. "Looking Behind the Scene in a Re-
     ligious Cult: Implications for the Study of Conver-
     sion." Sociological Analysis 41 (Summer): 137-43.
_____ and David Taylor. 1978. "On Getting in
     Tune: Some Reflections on the Process of Making
     Supernatural Contact." Paper presented at the an-
     nual meeting of the Pacific Sociological Associa-
     tion. Spokane, WA.
_____. 1977. "Seekers and Sauc-
     ers: The Role of the Cultic Milieu in Joining a
     UFO Cult." American Behavioral Scientist 20 July/
     August):839-60.
_____. 1976. "Salvation in a
     UFO." Psychology Today 10 (October):58-62, 66, 106.
Beckford, James. 1981. "'Brainwashing' and 'Deprogram-
     ming' in Britain: The Social Sources of Anti-Cult
     Sentiment." Forthcoming in James T. Richardson,
     ed., The Deprogramming Controversy: Sociological,
     Psychological, Legal and Historical Perspectives.
     New Brunswick, NJ: Transaction Books.
_____. 1978. "Accounting for Conversion." The
     British Journal of Sociology 29 (June): 249-62.
Bem, Daryl J. 1967. "Self Perception: An Alternative
     Interpretation of Cognitive Dissonance Phenomena."
     Psychological Review 74: 183-200.

_____. 1965. "An Experimental Analysis of Self-Persuasion." Journal of Social Psychology 1: 199-218.

Binder, Louis Richard. 1933. Modern Religious Cults and Society." New York: AMS Press.

Bowart, W.H. 1978. Operation Mind Control. New York: Dell.

Brinkerhoff, Merlin B. and Katheryn L. Burke. 1980. "Disaffiliation: Some Notes on 'Falling From the Faith.'" Sociological Analysis 41 (Spring): 41-54.

Bromley, David G., Bruce M. Busching, and Anson D. Shupe, Jr. 1980. "The Unification Church and the American Family: Strain, Conflict and Control." Paper presented at the annual meeting of the Society for the Scientific Study of Religion. Cincinnati, OH.

_____ and Anson D. Shupe, Jr. 1979a. "Moonies" in America: Cult, Church and Crusade. Beverly Hills, CA: Sage.

_____. 1979b. "'Just a Few Years Seem Like a Lifetime': A Role Theory Approach to Participation in Religious Movements." Pp. 159-85 in Louis Kriesberg, ed., Research in Social Movements, Conflicts and Change. Vol. 2, Greenwich, CT: JAI Press.

Casey, Robert P. 1941. "Transcient Cults." Psychiatry 4 (November): 525-34.

Clark, Jr., John G. 1979. "Cults." Journal of the American Medical Association 242 (July 20): 279-81.

Conway, Flo and Jim Siegelman. 1978. Snapping. New York: J.B. Lippincott.

Enroth, Ronald. 1979. The Lure of the Cults. Chappaqua, NY: Christian Herald Books.

_____. 1977. Youth, Brainwashing, and the Extremist Cults. Kentwood, MI: Zondervan.

Festinger, Leon, Henry W. Riecken and Stanley Schachter. 1964. When Prophecy Fails. New York: Harper Torchbooks.

Galenter, Marc, Richard Rabkin, Judith Rabkin, and Alexander Deutsch. 1979. "The Moonies: A Psychological Study of Conversion and Membership in a Contemporary Religious Sect." American Journal of Psychiatry 136 (February): 165-70.

Garrison, Vivian. 1974. "Sectarian and Psycho-social Adjustment: A Controlled Comparison of Puerto Rican Pentecostals and Catholics." Pp. 298-329 in Irving I. Zaretsky and Mark P. Leone, eds., Religious Movements in Contemporary America. Princeton, NJ: Princeton University Press.

Glock, Charles Y. 1964. "The Role of Deprivation in the Origin and Evolution of Religious Groups." In R. Lee and M.E. Marty, eds., Religion and Social Conflict. New York: Oxford University Press.

_____ and Rodney Stark. 1965. Religion and Society in Tension. Chicago: Rand McNally.

Heirich, Max. 1977. "Change of Heart: A Test of Some Widely Held Theories about Religious Conversion." American Journal of Sociology 83 (November): 653-80.

Hine, Virginia. 1974. "The Deprivation and Disorganization Theories of Social Movements." Pp. 646-61 in Irving I. Zaretsky and Mark P. Leone, eds., Religious Movements in Contemporary America. Princeton, NJ: Princeton University Press.

Hunter, Evan. 1962. Brainwashing: From Pavlov to Powers. New York: The Bookmailer.

_____. 1953. Brainwashing in Red China: The Calculated Destruction of Men's Minds. New York: Vanguard.

La Barre, Weston. 1972. The Ghost Dance. New York: Dell.

Levine, Saul V. and Nancy E. Salter. 1976. "Youth and Contemporary Religious Movements: Psychosocial Findings." Canadian Psychiatric Association Journal 21 (6): 411-20.

Lieberman, Seymour. 1956. "The Effects of Changes in Role on the Attitudes of Role Occupants." Human Relations 9 (4): 385-402.

Lifton, Robert. 1961. Chinese Thought Reform and the Psychology of Totalism. New York: Norton.

_____. 1956. "Thought Reform of Western Civilians in Chinese Communist Prison." Psychiatry 9: 385-402.

Lofland, John. 1977. "Becoming a World-Saver Revisited." American Behavioral Scientist 20 (July/August): 805-18.

_____. 1966. Doomsday Cult. Englewood Cliffs, NJ: Prentice-Hall.

_____ and Rodney Stark. 1965. "Becoming a World-Saver: A Theory of Conversion to a Deviant Perspective." American Sociological Review 30 (December): 862-74.

Lynch, Frederick R. 1977. "Toward a Theory of Conversion and Commitment to the Occult." American Behavioral Scientist 20 (July/August): 887-908.

Meerloo, J. 1956. The Rape of the Mind. New York: World.

Melton, J. Gordon. 1980. "What Really Happens When Prophecy Fails." Paper presented to the Conference on American Millenarianism. Unification Theological Seminary, Barrytown, NY.

Neal, Arthur A. 1970. "Conflict and the Functional Equivalence of Social Movements." Sociological Focus 3 (Spring): 3-12.

Richardson, James T. 1980. "Conversion Careers." Society 17 (March/April): 47-50.

_____. 1979. "A New Paradigm for Conver-
    sion Research." Paper presented at he 1979 meeting
    of the International Society for Political Psychol-
    ogy.

_____, Mary W. Stewart, and Robert B.
    Simmonds. 1979. Organized Miracles: A Study of a
    Contemporary Youth, Communal, Fundamentalist Organ-
    ization. New Brunswick, NJ: Transaction Press.

_____ and Mary Stewart. 1977. "Conversion
    Process Models and the Jesus Movement." American
    Behavioral Scientist 20 (July/August): 819-38.

Robbins, Thomas. 1979. Civil Liberties, "Brainwashing"
    and "Cults"--A Select Annotated Bibliography.
    Berkeley, CA: Program for the Study of New Religi-
    ous Movements in America.

_____ and Dick Anthony. 1979. "The Limits of
    'Coercive Persuasion' As an Explanation for Conver-
    sion to Authoritarian Sects." Paper presented to
    the annual meeting of the International Society
    of the International Society of Political Psycholo-
    gists. Washington, D.C. (Forthcoming in Political
    Psychology, 1980-81).

Sargent, William. 1957. Battle for the Mind. Garden City,
    NY: Doubleday.

Scheflin, Alan and Edward Opton. 1978. The Mind Manipul-
    ators. New York: Paddington.

Seggar, John and Philip Kuntz. 1972. "Conversion: Evalu-
    ation of a Step-Like Process for Problem-Solving."
    Review of Religious Research 13 (Spring): 178-84.

Shupe, Jr., Anson D. and David G. Bromley. 1980a. The
    New Vigilantes: Deprogrammers, Anti-Cultists and
    the New Religions. Beverly Hills, CA: Sage.

_____. 1980b. "A
    Role Theory Interpretation of Deprogramming." Paper
    presented at the annual meeting of the American
    Academy of Religion. Dallas, TX.

Shupe, Jr., Anson D., Roger Spielmann, and Sam Stigall. 1977. "Deprogramming: The New Exorcism." American Behavioral Scientist 20 (July/August):941-56.

Simmons, J.L. 1964. "On Maintaining Deviant Belief Systems: A Case Study." Social Problems 11 (Winter): 250-57.

Singer, Margaret T. 1979. "Coming Out of the Cults." Psychology Today 12 (January): 72-82.

Stark, Rodney and William Sims Bainbridge. 1980. "Networks of Faith: Interpersonal Bonds and Recruitment to Cults and Sects." American Journal of Sociology 85 (May): 1376-95.

Stoner, Carroll and Jo Anne Parke. 1977. All Gods Children. Radnor, PA: Chilton.

Straus, Roger A. 1978. "Some Notes on an Activist Paradigm for Religious Conversion and Its Underlying World View." Paper presented at the 1978 meeting of the Pacific Sociological Association. Spokane, WA.

Streiker, Lowell D. 1978. The Cults Are Coming! Nashville: Abingdon Press.

Ungerleider, J. Thomas. 1979. The New Religions: Insights Into the Cult Phenomenon. New York: Merck, Sharp and Dohms.

_____ and David Wellisch. 1979a. "Psychiatrists' Involvement in Cultism, Thought Control and Deprogramming." Psychiatric Opinion 16 (January): 10-15.

_____. 1979b. "Coercive Persuasion (Brainwashing), Religious Cults, and Deprogramming." American Journal of Psychiatry 136 (March): 279-82.

Verdier, Paul A. 1977. Brainwashing and the Cults. Hollywood, CA: Institute of Behavioral Conditioning.

Yinger, J. Milton. 1946. Religion in the Struggle for
    Power. Durham, N.C.: Duke University Press.
Zetterberg, Hans. 1952. "The Religious Conversion as
    a Change of Social Roles." Sociology and Social
    Research 36 (January/February): 159-66.

FURTHER SUGGESTED READING

Argyle, Michael. 1958. Religious Behavior. Glencone,
    IL: The Free Press.
Cantril, Hadley. 1941. The Psychology of Social Move-
    ments. London: Chapman and Hall.
Catton, Jr., William R. 1957. "What Kind of People Does
    a Religious Cult Attract?" American Sociological
    Review 22 (October): 561-66.
Downton, Jr., James V. 1979. Sacred Journeys: The Con-
    version of Young Americans to Divine Light Mission.
    New York: Columbia University Press.
Kim, Byong-suh. 1979. "Religious Deprogramming and Sub-
    jective Reality." Sociological Analysis 40 (Fall):
    197-207.
Mauss, Armand. 1969. "Dimensions of Religious Defection."
    Review of Religious Research 10 (Spring): 128-55.
Nock, A.D., 1933. Conversion. Oxford: The Clarenden
    Press.
Parrucci, Dennis J. 1968. "Religious Conversion: A The-
    ory of Deviant Behavior." Sociological Analysis
    29 (Fall): 144-54.
Stark, Rodney. 1971. "Psychopathology and Religious
    Commitment." Review of Religious Research 12
    (Spring): 165-76.
Zygmunt, Joseph F. 1972. "Movements and Motives: Some
    Unresolved Issues in the Psychology of Social Move-
    ments." Human Relations 25 (November): 449-87.

THOUGHTS FOR FURTHER CONSIDERATION

Is there some meeting point between social science models of conversion and faith maintenance and a religion's position that the convert has received a "call" from God? That is, does making reference to a convert's unhappy pre-conversion days automatically have to reduce or explain away the religious validity of his conversion? Many religious groups deliberately encourage converts to contrast their lives before and after they "found" Jesus, Krishna, the Lotus Sutra, Meher Baba, or a given guru as a way of validating the power for personal change inherent in their message. Yet psychological reductionistic approaches assume this power to always be in the eye of the self-selecting believer. How can a theology of conversion be constructed that is true both to what social science has learned of conversion processes and to the transcendent inspiration of religion?

THE SOCIAL STRUCTURAL PERSPECTIVE

The social structural perspective of fringe religions is a uniquely sociological one. That is, it focuses
at the organizational or group level, rather than on
the individual. Its concern is with recurrent patterns
of human interaction and exchange (what sociologists
term social structure), within fringe groups as well
as between such groups and their social environment(s).
Hence sociologists come to study a given group's
hierarchy of authority, recruitment practices, means
of social control over deviance or "heresy", and other
properties that any organization or "social system",
religious or secular, must necessarily possess. The social structural approach does not dispense with the subjective or cultural dimensions of a fringe religious
group's life, but while it may take into account the
theological beliefs of individual members it does so
always with the aim of linking these back to recurrent
observable patterns of behavior within the group. Thus
the group is conceptualized sociologically as an emergent entity that has a social significance greater than,
and distinct from, any individual members.[1]

Such an approach has been successfully used for
decades in examining the nonrandom structures and processes operating within mainline churches and denominations (see, e.g., Wood, 1970; Harrison, 1943), thus its
application to fringe religions is not terribly radical.
As in the research on conventional groups, the sociology

of fringe religions considers the distinct properties
of types of religious organization and how these types
evolve out of one another. In this sense the study of
such groups complements our knowledge of currently mainline "establishment" churches, since at one time all
of them were considered fringe by the cultures in which
they emerged.

Figure I presents a diagram illustrating the major
organizational types of fringe religions in an evolutionary process involving growth (size), differentiation
(internal complexity), and pluralism (variety). For
purposes of considering these types, the reader is ad-
vised to think of each as a possible stage in the life
of a single religion. No claim is made that there is
any natural history or inevitable pattern of development
which every religion follows. (About a similar model
of development, Wach 1967:154 made the disclaimer: "this
is not a simple 'one-line' development but is infinitely
more complex, involving reactions, reformations, and
counterreactions.") Indeed, we shall see that religious
evolution can follow various alternative routes. Thus
Figure I is merely a model, or ideal-type, to help illu-
minate organizational analysis. Before examining each
type or evolutionary stage in this model in terms of
sociological concepts, however, I want to consider
briefly what sociologists have to say about socio-
cultural conditions surrounding the birth of new religious movements.

SOCIAL ORIGINS OF NEW RELIGIONS

Sociologists tend to account for the emergence of
new religions as cultural innovations in one of two
ways. The first explanation is essentially the revitalization approach borrowed from anthropology without much

Figure 1

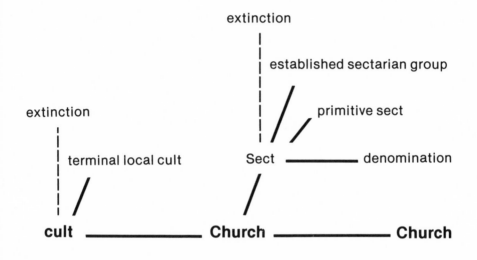

revision. Thus these fringe groups are perceived as revitalization movements attempting to help their alien-
ated or discontented members cope with the stress of
cultural change. For example, in a recent sociology of
religion text, Hargrove (1979:274) wrote of a "crisis
of confidence in modern Western culture" motivating
young seekers and concluded:

> There is a growing awareness in modern society
> that the basic assumptions of technical pro-
> gress and scientific knowledge may be leading
> not to Utopia but to a loss of humanity, if
> not total destruction. Not only this is so,
> but that awareness is compounded by the feel-
> ing that the technological machine cannot
> be stopped, that we are caught in an ever-
> descending spiral of our own making from which
> there is no escape.

Likewise, Eister (1974, 1972) saw cults arising
during times of dislocations or crises in the "communi-
cational and orientational institutions of advanced societies", i.e., in those institutions whose job it is
to provide and disseminate symbolic meaning about society, such as churches. Other studies making use of
these breakdown-revitalization assumptions to account
for the origins or spread of specific fringe groups,
such as the Divine Light Mission (Downton, 1979) and
the Unification Church (Bromley and Shupe, 1979; Robbins
et al., 1976), can easily be found. (I discussed the
revitalization approach in detail in "The Anthropological
Perspective.")

The second explanation assumes a permanent, perennial religious underground which at certain times re-
ceives more attention than at other times but which remains constant in its relative size. In other words,
it is our awareness of fringe religions' existence that

fluctuates more than their existence per se. Tiryakian (1972) calls this fringe stratum the realm of esoteric culture and notes its contributions to mainline belief and institutions, e.g., the contributions of ancient astrology and alchemy to astronomy and chemistry, respectively. Lofland (1966:69-70) in chronicling the efforts of the Unification Church to gain its first precarious missionary foothold in the United States in the early 1960s, saw the group as part of a subterranean "occult milieu", a subculture of "nebulous membership" pursuing metaphysics and other arcane topics generally ignored by both mainline churches and conventional colleges and universities. Wilson (1974:596) states this assumption of a constant deviant religious counterculture bluntly:

> Myriad religious sects, cults, and movements have populated American society throughout its history. To be sure, specific groups have developed and declined; probably the relative number of them, and the proportion of the poplation identified with them, however, have remained virtually constant for the better part of three centuries.

At this time it is difficult to decide conclusively which assumption is more valid. Undeniably most analysts of the current late twentieth century wave of new religions imply the revitalization model. This is not so much due to the fact that they are so close to the historical era being examined (though indeed they are part of it). Rather, while conceding that there exists at any given time some vaguely defined stratum of fringe religions, they would nevertheless maintain that periodically these groups expand or shrink (in size or number) according to other forces in the culture that affect their popular acceptance. The history of American religion (it could also be argued for western Christianity) has been one of revival/stabilization/decline-revival, and the fortunes of fringe groups in the religious underground correspondingly have ebbed and flowed.

THE CULT

There are two predominant usages of the term "cult". The first is cultural and reflects sociology's appropriation of the term from anthropology. A cultural definition of cult emphasizes the expression of religious devotion, reverence and faith through a set of beliefs and rituals, sometimes narrowly focusing attention on one aspect of a larger religious tradition. For example, in a popular sociology of religion text, O'Dea (1966:39) defined "cult" as "an acting out of feelings, attitudes, and relationships." Thus such analysts could speak of the cult of Osiris within larger archaic Egyptian religion or the cult of the Virgin Mary (sometimes called Mariolotry) within Roman Catholicism. "Cult" in this sense is an older, and was once a more commonly found use, of the term.

The second, more contemporary usage defines "cult" in structural terms, and it is from this perspective that I discuss cults here. A cult is conceptualized as the simplest level of religious organization, typically a religion at its earliest or most primitive stage before institutionalization and bureaucratization have occurred. For example, Washington (1973:158) defined a "cult" as

A new and syncretic religious movement in its early stages, emerging in alienation from a traditional religious system and society. In the beginning, it is characterized by small numbers, charismatic leadership, individual problem orientation, and presence in a local area. If it continues to exist and grow while society is undergoing drastic reorganization, the cult may involve itself with group as well as individual problems. At this juncture a new religion may develop with organization and doctrine, sectarian and churchly patterns.

Washington's definition closely resembles the generally accepted formulation of Nelson (1969) which I discussed in "Interpretations of Fringe Religions." Nelson's ideal-type definition has five points:

1. Cults tend to be short-lived. In most cases they go on to develop into larger religious movements and religions or meet extinction, though a few may remain in an indefinite state of "suspended animation", neither mustering the strength to expand nor expiring. (See the terminal local cults in Figure I.)

2. Cults tend to be loosely structured, with minimal organization and diffuse roles (rather than a division of labor). Usually they are centered around one or a few charismatic individuals. All decisions and organizational dilemmas are resolved (or at least confronted) by the leader, his immediate lieutenants, or the entire group in a collegiate, democratic fashion.

3. The individuals in the group tend to have had, or are in search of, ecstatic, mystical, or psychic experiences.[3]

4. The emphasis in the cult is on individual-oriented, rather than societal or extra-cult, problems. Therefore, by implication, cults are less often the vehicles for expressing blocked social mobility aspirations or channels of lower class protest.

5. Certainly as important as (2), <u>such groups make
a fundamental break with the dominant religious
tradition(s) of their host societies</u>. This is probably the single characteristic that most clearly
distinguishes between a cult and a sect (as we
shall see in a later section).

Most conventional world religions approached this
ideal-type at some point near their origins, e.g.,
Gautama Buddha and his first converts, or Mohammed and
his. The archetypal cult in western civilization would
be Jesus and his twelve disciples as well as the early
Christian church during the first century A.D. Theissen
(1978:8) points out that the "Jesus movement" (actually
a revitalization movement within ancient Judaism) spreading throughout Syria and Palestine from A.D. 30 to A.D.
70 lacked structure beyond local clusters of sympathetic
Jews and wandering charismatic leaders.

> The decisive figures in early Christianity
> were travelling apostates, prophets and dis-
> ciples who moved from place to place and could
> rely on small groups of sympathizers in these
> places. From the point of view of organiza-
> tion, these groups of sympathizers remained
> within the framework of Judaism. . . . It
> was. . .the homeless wandering charismatics
> who handed on what was later to take independ-
> ent form as Christianity. Use of the term
> 'charismatic' keeps in view the fact that
> their role was not an institutionalized form
> of life, a position which someone could adopt
> as a result of his own decision. The role of
> the charismatic is grounded in a call over
> which he had no control.

It was this period of minimal organizational structure,
oral (rather than written) tradition, and precarious
existence in an often hostile political milieu that laid

the groundwork for later Synoptic Gospels, theology, and conflict within the growing Christian movement.

Thus, structually speaking, the foundations of the cult initially rest on the relationship (often a dependent, highly emotional one) between a messiah/adept/seer and the group of his or her apprentice-pupils. While the latter may themselves possess measures of charismatic powers or occult skills independent of the Master, these are decidedly second class and only take on importance as they reflect the Master's uniqueness. They may ascend to fill the Master's leadership role when he or she is gone, but their inferior place in the primitive master/disciple stratification system is clear during the religion's initial formative period.

A final word on the character of the typical charismatic cult founder is in order. It is the vogue among critics of the current new religions in late twentieth century America not only to label all such fringe groups as cults, regardless of their frequent lack of similarity to the sociological model above, but also to impugn the motives of such groups' leaders and founders. Men such as the Unification Church's Sun Myung Moon or Hare Krishna's Bhaktivedanta Prabhupada are commonly castigated by the anti-cult movement as power-mad lunatics, charlatans, and insidious parasites. It is not my intention here to defend or refute such charges. However, the issue of the "real" qualities of cult leaders, whether genuinely occult and extraordinary or merely bogus and unexceptional, is from an organizational standpoint irrelevant. (Here I am obviously speaking from a structural, as opposed to an ethical, perspective.) As Kallen (1951:620) observed of religious leaders preaching certain radical truths:

> The creators or discoverers of these tech-
> niques need not themselves be convinced of
> them; their purposes may be altogether ulteri-
> or and their role may be to themselves that
> of swindlers and charlatans. This has no bear-
> ing on the success of their cults. These de-
> pend not at all on the moral character of the
> founders but on the credited function of the
> cults among their communicants, on the sense
> of present security and well-being and cer-
> tainty of ultimate salvation which they estab-
> lish.

In other words, the determinants of a movement's fate
are better located in its modes of operation and structural qualities instead of in its founder's presumed
psychological and moral states.

THE CULT IN TRANSITION

Cults do not inevitably survive to become churches.
Indeed, to paraphrase Pareto, history is the graveyard
of religions. One can count on the fingers of a single
hand the number of cults successfully meeting the challenges of long-range survival to become major world religions. Such slim odds facing any cult suggest some
factors crucial to group growth beyond simply the optimism and aspirations of most infant religions.

From a structural perspective, a necessary (though
not solely sufficient) requirement for any cult to survive is its ability to organize in an efficient manner
relations within the membership and between the members
and the wider social environment. It is more than plausible, for example, that early Christianity alone, of
its many rivals and contemporaries in the late Hellen-
istic era, accomplished these basic organizational prerequisites. At any rate, while growth and expansion may

still remain problematic for an organizationally sound religion, it is unlikely that any group could go forward for very long without having resolved the following major problems:

1. SUCCESSION. Wach (1967:137) observed: "The immediate crisis which marks the birth of a new epoch in the development of the infant religion and causes its structural transformation is the death of its founder." Whereas the cult had been composed of a charismatic leader and a more or less equal band of disciples (or "circle", in Wach's terms), the former's death suddenly poses a leadership crisis. Wach referred to the "brotherhood" as the intermediate stage of a religion between the role-diffuse, basically astructural cult and more complex organizational forms. The brotherhood is a band of equals who must suddenly choose one among them to stand in the place of the "irreplaceable". Questions that immediately confront disciples must be answered if the brotherhood is not to disintegrate: HOW SHALL WE CARRY ON? WHO SHALL REPLACE THE MASTER AND MAKE HIS DECISIONS? WHAT SHOULD BE HIS QUALIFICATIONS?

In the event that the founder, before his death, designates his successor or the procedure of selection, the brotherhood is less apt to be torn apart by possible conflicting claims of succession. The likelihood of schisms that can weaken the cult's precarious solidarity also decreases if the brotherhood reaches a consensus as to selection procedures.

This dilemma may actually be more acute in the second or third generation than during the brotherhood period. Even within the rough equality of the original disciples there may be some "pecking order" or favoritism shown toward the more charismatic and/or original ones (such as Simon Peter in the early Jesus movement) that elevates them above the rest as natural candidates

for the role of successor. Aside from the likelihood
of greater doctrinal consensus among the original disciples, the powers passed on from the founder also flow
to a small pool of potential leaders. Later, however,
when these first disciples themselves have died, or when
conversion has swelled the membership ranks, there will
be more opportunities for counter-charismatics or schis-
matics to reinterpret the founder's doctrines or to
claim some revelation of equal legitimacy without a
challenge from those who intimately knew the founder.
In other words, the awe of the originators that could
have discouraged deviations will have disappeared.

2. OBJECTIFICATION. The German sociologist Simmel
(1950:352ff) spoke of the "sociology of the letter" and
its effects on a community of believers. By the "sociology of the letter" Simmel meant that in the beginning
the leader of a small group inspires believers, rein-
forces their commitment and controls their behavior
largely through strong emotional bonds grounded in face-
to-face interaction. In other words, the cult is what
sociologists conventionally term a "primary group".

However, for a variety of reasons it becomes necessary to turn initially emotionally felt truths into
written standardized form, to objectify them in symbols
and rituals. This is imperative for socialization, especially as time removes new members further and further
from the lives of the founder(s) and disciples. While
at its primitive stages several succeeding generations
of a cult can memorize and orally pass on ethical truths
along with the emotional contexts to emboss them, sheer
membership size as the cult expands threatens to encourage different versions of truth (particularly if the
founder was geographically mobile and scattered bits
of oral wisdom, rarely recorded in any form, wherever
he or she went). Missionaries need texts to which they

can refer and worshippers need a common frame of reference for communal services. Memories can fail. A theological tradition has difficulty growing if it is not written down. Standard scriptures may become seen as functional to settle once and for all doctrinal disputes or to point to for prestige.

Thus, because of these pressures, objection becomes a necessary evil, but sometimes members perceive the evil as outweighing the necessity. The printed words and rituals often do not convey the inspiration of the spirit. What O'Dea (1966:94-5) termed "the dilemma of delimitation", i.e., rendering the original mystical message into practical mundane forms for use in daily life, takes place much to the chagrin of the more subjectively and idealistically inclined believers. O'Dea terms this a dilemma because as a process objectification appears to be unavoidable (as Simmel would have no doubt agreed) if the cult is to expand beyond the brotherhood stage, yet at the same time it remains as a potential source of alienation and dissatisfaction to some. The Montanist schism in the second century Christian church, for example, was essentially a protest against the early codified formality of worship. The Montanists' wish to draw back into a more emotionally gratifying charismatic style could be interpreted as a revolt against encroaching delimitation.

Part of the challenge confronting the primitive religious organization, then, is to accomplish this objectification of beliefs for the sake of the general membership while providing some avenue for the intellectuals and mystics to express and cultivate precisely that which objectification partially destroys. Objectification implies a tension that may never be completely resolved.

3. ROLE DIFFERENTIATION. A third development necessary for expansion of the cult is the division of labor
within the group. As the cult grows in size the same
emotional attachments that worked to produce order and
consensus in a face-to-face situation no longer suffice.
Personal interaction between leader and each follower
becomes, in structural terms, a technological impossibility. Jesus could maintain some social control over
the thoughts and behaviors of the twelve disciples when
they numbered only twelve and roamed through the coun-
tryside of Palestine, divorced from the many mundane
complexities incurred by working and raising families
on a day-to-day basis. Had they numbered twelve thousand
during Jesus' lifetime and been often out of his sight
and direct influence for much of the time, a different
basis for order to ensure "correct" thoughts would have
been imperative.

Cult growth means that someone must supervise the
rituals and administer sacraments that inevitably develop out of objectification. The duties of leading worship
expand to become a full-time specialty. Training of
these specialists becomes mandatory. Persons whose task
it is to interpret and study the emerging scriptures,
or at least to reproduce them in whatever form, must
be supported. Eventually someone else must teach and
supervise these functionaries, while someone else again
will have to maintain the records on contributions,
rents, salaries, and, perhaps, taxes. Births will occur
or at least new converts must be enumerated, and they
must be not only registered but taught. If the cult be-
lieves in proselytizing its message, there must be
trained proselytizers and coordinators, perhaps trans-
lators as well. Responsibilities and duties, in short,
will have to be differentially assigned to handle the

work loads emerging due to the increase in group size and doctrinal complexity.

Role differentiation is the inescapable result of growth, and many of the impersonal characteristics of successful religions are the direct products of cults aggressively pursuing their idealistic goals. Succession, objectification, and role differentiation are actually separate dimensions of a more general process which Weber (1964:398) termed the "routinization of charisma", i.e., where the unique powers of an individual become translated into organizational forms and impersonal bureaucracy comes to replace cultic style. In his often cited statement on charisma Weber defined it as

> A certain quality of an individual personality
> by virtue of which he is set apart from or-
> dinary men and treated as endowed with super-
> natural, superhuman, or at least specifically
> exceptional powers or qualities. These are
> such as are not accessible to the ordinary
> person, but are regarded as of divine origin
> or as exemplary, and on the basis of them the
> individual concerned is treated as a leader.

Moreover, Weber conceptualized this original personal charisma as basically incompatible with organizations and bureaucracy. Charismatic authority tends to be non-economic or opposed to mundane routine in the sense that it bases its claims to regulate, not on established patterns of rationality, efficiency or tradition, but rather on the direct inspiration of the extraordinary individual leader. To the extent that an individual can command others and give them as a rationale for obedience his or her own inspiration, charisma has an arbitrary noninstitutionalized nature.

However, the perceived personal qualities of a leader, tied as they are to personality, alone do not constitute a stable basis for permanent growth. In the long run the majority of followers will never know the leader-founder or perhaps ever see the latter. Most followers will need to leave transcendental heights and face the gritty problems of daily existence: earning a living, reproducing, and interacting in a world filled with nonbelievers. The institution-shattering orientation of the charismatic leader is perhaps functional for overthrowing the old order, but, like the electrical principle behind a lightning bolt, its power must be harnessed if anything useful is to be gained from it. "Perpetual revolutions" as a philosophy can only occur within some minimally ordered structure or system, or else such revolutions become meaningless. There is also the impracticality, and even impossibility, of expecting all persons to drop totally and permanently their secular responsibilities to go and become "fishers of men". As in political revolutions, frenetic anti-institutional activity can go on only so long before a "thermidor" or emotional burn-out occurs, and then a search for more stable patterns, with their own unique satisfactions, begins.

Thus, Weber felt that over time the burning emotionalism behind charisma would be subject to pressures to become routinized, to be channeled into some form more compatible with the economic and social realities of secular existence. Successful routinization can therefore be interpreted as the bureaucratization of a cult: solving problems of administration and passing on leadership power; standardizing beliefs, molding them into a more easily transmittable symbolic form (such as scriptures), and defining heresy; and setting up structures or positions for socializing new members, accounting for resources, and so forth. Charisma may survive, but it must remain under the control of the organization, not any single individual.

This process has occurred not only in major world religions such as Christianity but also in such recent groups as the Unification Church (Bromley and Shupe, 1979) The Church of Jesus Christ of Latter-Day Saints (Durham, 1942) and Daddy Grace's United House of Prayer. Weber gave examples of cases where procedures for selecting persons to fill awe-inspiring positions had been standardized. For example, one of these was the "charisma of office", really a more specific type of the "charisma of ritual", such as occurs when powers are bestowed on persons (such as priests) through holy orders and ordination or (such as kings) through coronation. Eisenstadt (1968:xxi) has remarked that Weber's recognition of such standardized, organizationally controllable charisma

> indicates that the test of any great charismatic leader lies not only in his ability to create a single event or great movement, but also in his ability to leave a continuous impact on an institutional structure--to transform any given institutional setting by infusing into it some of his charismatic vision, by investing the regular, orderly offices, or aspects of social organization seems to be obliterated--to be revived again only in situations of extreme and intensive social disorganization and change.

In sum, the transition from cult to church organization can occur only when personal charisma is transformed into an attribute of some office (and by association, the officeholder) in the religious group. The fact that so few religious cults in history have survived

can be sociologically accounted for by their failure
to accomplish this basic requirement.

Or the obvious alternative may occur. The cult dies
out. Such dissolution or near dissolution can occur for
any one of numerous reasons. The leader may lose his
or her charisma or be discredited in the eyes of followers. This happened in 1974 when Guru Maharaj Ji, the
Hindu teenage "Perfect Master" of the Divine Light Mission, married his secretary (an older American woman)
in a civil ceremony that led many DLM members to recon-
sider their own austere lifestyles and caused the Guru's
mother to denounce her son's leadership role in the international movement. Though the Divine Light Mission
did not pass out of the American scene, this loss of
the Guru's esteem decimated the ranks of his followers
in the United States; from an estimated 50,000 members
nationwide before the marriage to less than 6,000 after
(see Pilarzyk, 1978), turning it into what I shall
shortly discuss as a "terminal cult".

Or extreme persecution by agents of social control
may discourage recruiting of new members or impair the
cult's operations until such time as it withers away
into obscurity. This eventually happened with one particularly revolting group beside which anything seen
in twentieth century America's wave of new religions
pales: the Skopzi (in Russian, the "castrated"). The
Skopzi originated in a wave of eighteenth and nineteenth
century penitentiary/masochistic religious sects sweep-
ing Czarist Russia. Some, such as the Siberian
Soshigateli ("the Self-Burners") claimed suicide by fire
was the sole means to cleanse personal sin. Believers
would immolate themselves in large pits or buildings
filled with kindling. (In 1867 alone approximately 1700
persons did themselves in by this method.) Another
group, the Morelstschiki ("the Self-Sacrificers")

considered it a sacred duty to kill each other for religious atonement. The limited longevity of these two fringe groups is obvious. Members of the Skopzi, a group caught up in this same amazing obsession with self-multilation, lacerated their genitals with red-hot irons, knives, razors, hatchets, and glass (both males and females) and for a time virtually defied frantic attempts by the government to stamp them out. Put in jails, they converted their jailers. Locked away in monasteries, they converted the monks. All social classes participated in the movement, including priests, merchants, military officers, peasants, and nobles. By 1874 the number of persons having undergone "conversion" was conservatively estimated to be at least 5444. Ultimately, ruthless repression and mass deportation to obscure corners of the empire (plus the obvious fact that believers depended on conversions rather than reproduction for new members) brought about an end to the Skopzi's grisly rites (see Hackethorn, 1965:292-300).

Another reason for the cult's demise may be because the founder claimed all charisma for all time, pretended immortality, or so completely discouraged thought of eventual succession problems after his death that followers are unable to organize. An example was the Peace mission cult centered around Father Divine in the 1930s and 1940s which I discussed in "The Criminological Perspective." Divine, a black charismatic who claimed to be God Incarnate, was credited with miraculous powers and inspired the idea of his own immortality and of all true believers in his movement. As one participant observer wrote:

> What is to occur should anything happen to Father Divine is an unintelligible question to any follower in the movement. Nothing can happen to Father Divine. He will never die; he is God. (Fauset, 1970:62)

Likewise, Harris (1971:343) noted: "Father Divine is too profound a believer in his own philosophy to make plans for dying. Since he knows he will live forever, he does not think about successors for his movement." The failure to develop any organization capable of carrying on minus its founder, coupled with an absolute belief in the indestructibility of Father Divine, led to the rapid demoralization and disintegration of the Peace Mission Movement soon after Divine's predictable death.

On the other hand, the movement of a similar black messianic figure of the pre-World War II years, Bishop Charles Emmanuel "Daddy" Grace (who also claimed divinity, at least indirectly) did not expire with him. Grace's uncouth flamboyance, particularly his claim that he had ordered God to "take a vacation," had a magnetic appeal in drawing poor urban blacks into his cult. Grace ran a monolithic organization with a tight personal rein on all its aspects, particularly the appointment of preachers and finances. He did allow a constitution, bylaws, and a General Council of Elders for the United House of Prayer, but as Robinson (1974:215) noted,

> The constitution was not thorough in specify-
> ing the electoral procedure for a successor
> to Daddy. Hence, turmoil erupted within the
> organization upon Daddy's death.

With Grace gone the church elders elected one of their ministers, Walter McCullough, to the supreme office of bishop (he became "Sweet Daddy Grace McCullough") but factions within the United House of Prayer sued on the grounds that the election was illegal. In later court actions a District Court judge deposed McCullough. A reelection was held and McCullough won easily. McCullough subsequently revised Grace's old constitution into a more coherent framework and initiated a ministerial school to replace Grace's former arbitrary practice of personally ordaining church leaders. Thus Robinson (1974:233) concluded:

> It is common for cults to disintegrate upon the death of their leader. However, the genius of Daddy Grace provided, even though ambiguously, for a successor. Although Bishop McCullough, the successor, lacks the religious charisma and originality of Daddy Grace, both his tenacity in pursuing legal action and his organizational ability have given stability to the movement.

While Daddy Grace's organizational "genius" might be questioned, he did at least anticipate a time when leadership of the United House of Prayer would have to be assumed by someone else. This case also doubtlessly illustrates the critical importance of having dimensions of a religious movement within the brotherhood corps.

THE CHURCH

When cults survive and do not fade into extinction, they face one of two possible futures. The first is an uncertain, indefinite existence as a "terminal cult". The terminal cult manages just barely to sustain itself with members and other resources, never enough to expand and develop beyond the cultic stage but yet enough to persist over time. Since such a state is usually the result of a delicate balance of forces both within and outside the cult, dependent on such unpredictable factors as leaders' tenacity or a supply of rich elderly widows, terminal cults maintain a precarious foothold in society. Such groups as the flying saucer enthusiasts researched by Buckner (1968), for example, manifest structural and doctrinal qualities that prevent them

from evolving out of this condition. Buckner found mod-
est-sized groups that were extremely eclectic and toler-
ant of members' beliefs (no matter how outlandish), even
adopting norms against demanding orthodoxy. This open-
ended tolerance attracted many persons with strong con-
victions on esoteric topics ranging from spirit survival
to lost continents, but it also held the firm commitment
of few. Any attempt by a group meeting under the general
auspices of interest in flying saucers that attempted
to tighten up control over members or seek closure in
its beliefs would immediately drive members elsewhere.
As a general rule, terminal cults can be distinguished
from simple cults only on the basis of their relative
longevity.

The second alternative course of development is
the "church". The church is the established cult: sur-
viving its environmental challenges and prospering; out-
living both its rivals as well as its former oppressive
state religion; succeeding in becoming the mainline religion, no longer regarded simply as a band of bizarre
believers; trading its "exotic" reputation for one of
respectabilty. The church is now legitimate where the
cult was illegitimate.

The classic statement on the church-type was that
of Ernst Troeltsch (1960), a pupil of Max Weber, who
analyzed the history of Christianity. For Troeltsch,
the church-type was something other than what the ordinary meaning of church has become in pluralistic American
society. Troeltsch wrote of the universal church, the
Roman Catholic church of western civilization, the
single mainline religion of a society that had so completely compromised its originally revolutionary principles that its leaders were intimately involved in secular roles and affairs (enjoying the latters' temptations and privileges) while simultaneously maintaining

ecclesiastical authority. The church assumed that all members of a society were ipso facto also members of the church. Indeed, membership was automatic at birth. Religious grace came as the consequence of conformity with approved objectified (ritualistic) activity rather than through subjective experience. Religious heresy became a political crime. In sum, what others since Troeltsch have treated as an ideal-type church was to Troeltsch a construct grounded in the history of the medieval Roman Catholic church.

It is obvious that the universalistic church of Troeltsch's analysis is not the church of modern American experience. While the first colonies did establish state-supported churches patterned after the European experience, they never had the scope or broad cultural support necessary to maintain their hold on secular affairs that the Catholic Church had possessed in the old world. Troeltsch's church was a pervasive, culturally omnipresent institution with a single hierarchy and theology. It makes little sense to talk in terms of an American church, not only because our religious organizations exist in a pluralistic society where no one group is dominant or commands a majority of members, but also because these groups exist in a more sharply delimited social environment. Their influence is curtailed to the extent that they have become simply another type of interest association in competition for political influence. We have no single religious hierarchy with the secular influence, size, and moral authority corresponding to the church's in medieval Christendom.

There are costs associated with the success of the cult's transformation into a church. O'Dea (1966:90-97) delineated these as five "dilemmas of institutionalization" that cause many of the church's "internal strains and functional problems":

The Dilemma of Mixed Motivation results from the
growth in various career opportunities within the components of the church and the gradual transformation
of goals and values among church leaders. O'Dea noted:

> When a professional clergy emerges in the
> church, there comes into existence a body of
> men for whom the clerical life offers not sim-
> ply the "religious" satisfactions of the ear-
> lier charismatic period, but also prestige
> and respectability, power and influence, in
> both church and society, and satisfactions
> derived from the use of personal talents in
> teaching, leadership, etc. (89)

Whereas the first disciples joined the cult with rather
single-minded purposes, the church offers a host of at-
tractions to various persons. Consequently the church's
actual operation comes to reflect these mixed motives.

The Symbolic Dilemma: Objectification versus Alienation is a central problem discussed earlier in this
chapter. The letter is a poor substitute for the spirit
for many in the future generations following the cult
stage. O'Dea notes: "The symbol loses its power to
elicit and affect attitudes and emotions. Objectification, necessary for continuity, leads finally to alienation." (92)

The Dilemma of Administrative Order: Elaboration
and Alienation comes with the increases in sheer size
and structural complexity of the church. New offices
and roles have to be created to cope with challenging
needs. However, O'Dea says,

> Structures which emerge in one set of condi-
> tions and in response to one set of problems
> may turn out later to be unwieldy instruments
> for handling new problems under new condi-
> tions. (93)

One associated problem is that because of mixed motivation officials and members develop vested interests in maintaining aspects of the church as it is while other sections of the church may clamor for change. Such self-interest can alienate the church structure (i.e., inhibit its responsiveness) from contemporary social problems and cause a gap between officials and rank and file members, as some critics of the Roman Catholic Church's formal policies on birth control and divorce have argued that it has done.

The Dilemma of Delimitation: Concrete Definition versus Substitution of the Letter for the Spirit is similar to the problem of objectification but deals more with the church's persistent tendency to work out the cult's original ethical insight in prosaic, day-to-day matters. In this way church doctrine becomes elaborated and turns into "a vast intellectual structure which serves not to guide the faith of untrained specialists but rather to burden it." (95) Religious inspiration thus turns into dry legalism that regulates or even oppresses daily life.

Finally, the Dilemma of Power: Conversion versus Coercion has underlain some of the bloodiest religious wars in European history as well as the persecution of religious minorities in American history. Originally the cult's disciples were "called" to their new religion. The faith of later generations, however, largely inherited tradition supported by the taken-for-granted social reality of family, friends, and reinforcing public opinion. Religious faith becomes "accepted without examination". Moreover, the church's comfort with the secular society means that the religious leaders come to equate their respective goals with society's. They "tend to rely upon social consensus and even on legal authority to buttress and supplement voluntary adherence." (96)   Thus the spontaneous, voluntary character of religion can turn into state-enforced conformity.

O'Dea's five dilemmas encroach on any religious organization of any size and duration.   Their sum effect is to alienate believers, to guarantee factional disputes and discontent, and therefore to stimulate religious conflict.   The fact that these dilemmas are never completely resolved explains the perennial emergence of sects.

SECTS AND DENOMINATIONS

Troeltsch's sect-type was the opposite of the church-type, a group defecting from established universal Christendom.   Such groups were essentially movements of protest against the corruption and worldliness that developed with the church's unbridled participation in secular affairs and its overreliance on rituals, formulas and sacraments as the means to grace.   In consequence, sects attempted a self-conscious imitation of "primitive" or "pure" Christianity at its lowest institutionalized state.   Membership was voluntary (by conversion) rather than ascribed at birth, grace was achieved by inner direct experience and personal ethical behavior outside institutional sacraments, bureaucracy and hierarchy were abandoned in favor of a "priesthood of all believers", and strong primary group bonds among members sustained this orientation against persecution and temptation to return to the "world".   Moreover, as with the cult, a charismatic leader frequently began the defection process.

Marxian tradition maintains (in true economic reductionist fashion) that religious protest is merely political protest against oppressive class conditions translated into religious or metaphysical terms.   The influence of this view can be found in various sociological treatments of sects, both classical (such as the Methodists, Baptists, and Quakers) and contemporary ones. Thus Stark (1967:5) writes of the sect: "It is a kind of protest movement, distinguished from other similar movements by the basic fact that it experiences and expresses its dissatisfactions and strivings in religious (rather than political or economic or generally secular) terms." Clark (1949:16) also sees basic lower-class antagonisms inherent in sect movements:

> Finding themselves ill at ease in the presence of an effete and prosperous bourgeoisie, their emotional natures unsatisfied by a middle-class complacency, their economic problems disregarded by those who have no such problems to meet, and their naive faith and simple interpretations smiled upon by their more cultured fellows, the poor and ignorant revolt and draw apart into groups which are more congenial.

There have been explicit reactions against this Marxist view of sects' origins (which was developed with Protestant Reformation sects in mind) by sociologists such as Wach (1967:203).[4] Nevertheless, it has influenced much of the existing church-sect literature. American sociology, with its strong empirical orientation, has been preoccupied with examining the characteristics of members of nonmainline groups designated as sects. This research, intended to clarify church and sect types, has resulted in an enormous and bewildering collection of statistical correlates and noncorrelates that point to many (though not all) sect adherents as sharing some lower class characteristics or has produced essays arguing why they should have those characteristics. Critics of this approach (see, e.g., Goode, 1967a,

1967b; Eister, 1967) have argued that confusion of specific historical sects with the more theoretical sects
ideal-type had throughly muddied the waters in understanding the dynamics of sect formation. They claim that
the church-sect dichotomy has outlived its original purpose, i.e., to further analytical understanding, and
caused confusion for researchers trying to fit real
groups to the ideal-type or continually tinkering with
the ideal-type each time an exception is discovered.
All this, they add, consumes needless space in professional journals without advancing sociology. Greeley
(1972:78) advocated abandoning the jungle of complex
redefinitions and counterelaborations grown up around
the concept of sect in favor of simply applying already
abundant hypotheses in the area of formal organization.

For our purposes here it is essential only to note
the two critical dimensions on which sects differ from
cults in order to retain the value of distinguishing
cults, churches, and sects. First, while cults are eclectic religious movements that put together their own
innovative theologies, sects are splintering-off reform
movements within an established religious tradition.
The Protestant sects of the Reformation, for instance,
simply sought to relive the nonroutinized charismatic
experience of prebureaucratic, premainline Christianity.
They did not create their scriptures anew. Second, cults
have a loose definition of membership and correspondingly vague criteria for proper belief whereas sects
tend toward exclusiveness in membership (they often consider themselves spiritual elites), and they define
themselves as they go; sects know their tradition and
possess identities in terms of it.

The final alternative stages or types in our evolutionary model correspond to possible outcomes of sect
development.   Some sects, particularly if they take

deliberate steps to isolate themselves from exchange and social intercourse with outsiders (developing what sociologists call "norms of avoidance"), may remain minimally affected by larger society and preserve their primitive exclusionary goals. Such groups as various Amish and Mennonite orders, through cultivation of dialects and taboos on "worldly" clothing, automobiles, and so forth, have accomplished this more or less. Other sectarian groups, like the Mormons or the Christian Scientists, have maintained fewer exclusionary norms, integrated more with mainline society, but nevertheless because of lifestyle and doctrinal demands successfully retained some sectarian distinctiveness. These are termed established sectarian groups.

Other sects, in spite of their initial intentions, turn into the very things they seek to be different from: church-like structures called denominations. Just as the revolutionary Jesus movement of ancient Palestine evolved into the medieval Roman Catholic Church, these Protestant sects have undergone or are undergoing Weber's routinization of charisma and become/are becoming institutionalized. They overcame the same obstacles as the first Christian cult once did and survived. The very values of thrift, sobriety, and cohesiveness which sects have maintained to distinguish themselves from the "fallen, secular" world are the same ones that increase their odds of prosperity and upward social mobility.[5] The latter in turn increase the probability of compromise and "worldly infection". Niebuhr (1929) referred to this transformation of sects as "denominationalization". Here it is important only to reiterate that the social sources of denominations are the same as those that produce churches out of cults. The prerequisites of organizational growth, doctrinal elaboration, and concrete success in dealing with the socio-political environment place the same undeniable pressures on both cults and sects.[6]

THE CULT-TO-SECT-PHENOMENON

The model of organizational evolution in Figure I represents the sequence of organizational changes in a religious tradition as generally conceived by sociologists. Recently, however, a number of studies based on data taken from such diverse fringe religious groups as the flying saucer cult of Bo and Peep, the Divine Light Mission, and Scientology have suggested that cults may bypass much of this development process and be transformed directly into sects through a process of "sectarianization". The catalyst for such change seems to be the charismatic leader's desire to obtain greater organizational coherence and cohesiveness. Sectarianization is largely accomplished through centralizing the leader's authority over members and defining the boundaries of ideological orthodoxy.

Wallis (1977, 1974) has preeminently championed the existence of such a transformation, particularly through his study of Scientology. Scientology began as Dianetics in the 1950s, born of the inspiration of science-fiction writer L. Ron Hubbard. After a brief faddish popularity that resulted in a decentralized movement composed of local cells essentially autonomous of any organizational control other than themselves, Hubbard reasserted his claims to unique knowledge and began to consolidate the movement into Scientology (see the First Case in this chapter), resulting in a much more authoritarian, centralized organization.

Wallis' definition of a cult is organizational and similar to the one developed by Nelson which I have employed here. His main difference from Nelson's definition is that he maintains there is no predominant locus of authority analogous to the central charismatic leader which Nelson posits. Wallis says the cult is deviant, loosely structured, with tolerance for a wide variety of beliefs and doctrinal variations, i.e., its beliefs are poorly distinguished from those of other groups in the "cultic milieu". It is a fragile institution that holds weak commitment from its members. As a group it has precarious existence. Alternately, the sect is authoritarian, with specifically defined beliefs and "clear" leadership. Wallis dismisses many of the other characteristics normally associated with sects (such as achieved membership status, asceticism, or egalitarian relations among members) as merely "a consequence of historical circumstances in which religious protest was legitimated by an appeal to the presumed characteristics of the early church, and not part of a universal characterization of sectarianism." (1974:302) In other words, the classic protesting sects of European history deliberately imitated their understanding of what primitive Christianity was about, but these groups represented only one possible example of general sectarian phenomena. (This criticism is similar to those of other social scientists unhappy with the western history-bound use of the entire church-sect dichotomy.)

Sectarianization is therefore the process of constructing "epistemological authoritarianism", that is, of tightening up an otherwise loose organization. It involves the "arrogation of authority." Says Wallis:

> Sects possess some authoritative locus for the legitimate attribution of heresy. Sects lay a claim to possess unique and privileged access to the truth or salvation. Their committed adherents typically regard all those outside the confines of the collectivity as "in error." The truth must be protected from

defilement or misuse and therefore extensive
control is necessary over those to whom access
is permitted, and the exclusion of the un-
worthy. (1977:17)

Other research has incorporated this model.
Pilarzyk (1978) examined how Guru Maharaj Ji transformed
the former doctrinal and organizational laxness of the
Divine Light Mission in 1974 after a rift developed in
the movement between the Guru and his family in India,
and Balch and Taylor (1977) reported on sectarianization
in the nomadic Bo and Peep UFO cult after the flying
saucer(s) failed to transport believers elsewhere in
the universe and the group assumed a more permanent residence. In addition, Richardson (1979) has elaborated
on the theory beyond sectarianization. This evidence
suggests that the process which Wallis described is real.

But are we seeing cults turn directly into sects?
Or are we merely witnessing the cult's coming to grips
with the same traditional problems and obstacles which
I noted above? Earlier in this chapter, I discussed
succession, objectification, and role differentiation.
Certainly there are other organizational requisites
and succession has not even yet had to be faced in any
of the groups researched by Wallis, Pilarzyk, or Balch
and Taylor. THE DEFINITIONS OF ORTHODOXY AND CENTRALI-
ZATION/ELABORATION OF AUTHORITY SEEM TO ME TO BE CON-
SISTENT WITH THE ROUTINIZATION PROCESS TRANSFORMING A
CULT INTO A CHURCH. The fact that both cult and sect
forms of the groups studied by these authors are deviant
simply suggests their close proximity still to the cult
stage. After all, Christianity spent several centuries
as a deviant, persecuted group, yet the sectarianization
changes of which Wallis and others write began occuring
in that cult by the end of the first century A.D. For
example, the loose, collegiate structure of the early
Christian movement with elders or presbyters electing

bishops in local congregations was replaced around 100 A.D. by the "monarchial episcopate" (bishops had to be ordained by other bishops) and hierarchy began quickly to replace the older democratic style. Likewise, the largely oral traditions plus Pauline letters and whatever early versions of the Gospel of Mark (and its vanished precursors that had been available) had, by the early second century A.D. pyramided into a fairly substantial literature of competing gospels, some eventually judged apocryphal, some gnostic, and others legitimate. (See, among the many available sources, Walker, 1970; Hughes, 1949; Latourette, 1937.)

My point is simply that sectarianization as cult-to-sect transformation seems the same institutionalization process as the cult-to-church one, and that what we consequently are seeing is not a sect produced at all but rather an embryonic, growing structure assuming shape on its way to (but with no guarantees of) becoming a church. To adopt the Wallis et al. usage of the term "sect" also deprives it of its meaning as a protest-reform movement that splinters off from a mainline religious institution. I do not consider this as irrelevant a characteristic as some of the others with which Wallis dispensed in his reformulation.

In this chapter I have doubtlessly left non-sociologists with the impression that the primary concern of sociologists in their studies of fringe religions is always structural. This, however, is far from the case. Many sociologists are concerned with the more general cultural meaning of the appearance of fringe religions (e.g., Foss and Larkin, 1979; Glock and Bellah, 1976), which leads them much closer to the mutual concerns of anthropologists and liberal philosophers.

Others search for patterns in the characteristics of seekers and adherents (see Wuthnow, 1978), which in turn may also reveal general qualities about our society. I have chosen to present the social structural view of fringe religions and quite consciously equated it with the sociological perspective precisely because it is uniquely sociological. Sociology is the study of aggregate and group patterns, of how numerous individuals create structure and regularity out of their interactions. While there are numerous, various specific ways in which a sociologist might approach a fringe religion for analysis, it would still be with this general supraindividual focus in mind.

CASE STUDIES

The following pair of studies concerns two of the best publicized fringe religions in the cult controversy of the 1970s and 1980s: Scientology and the Unification Church. Both books attempt to reconstruct the organizational development of the respective groups through the use of interviews, observations, and documents. Both books are also more than simply descriptions of this development process. They are guided by a larger interest in fleshing out the general sociological principles from intensive case studies and thereby contribute to the sociological theory of social movements.

FIRST CASE

The Road to Total Freedom:
A Sociological Analysis of Scientology
Roy Wallis

Wallis' study is a rags-to-riches story of the birth, faddish acceptance, subsequent stagnation, eventual rejuvenation, and aggressive expansion of a cult. The cult began as Dianetics, the brainchild of science-fiction writer L. Ron Hubbard, and spread quickly during the early 1950s. Without a coherent organizational structure to guide its development or monitor and prevent heresy, however, the early movement began to unravel and go in different directions at once according to the separate visions of Hubbard's followers. Hubbard therefore began to centralize control of the movement in mid-decade, changing the name to the Church of Scientology, establishing criteria for certification, weeding out heretics (and thereby defining orthodoxy), and extending the doctrines prolifically.

Much of this centralization, at least by Wallis' account and the evidence he presents, appears to have been undertaken by Hubbard with a certain ruthlessness. Those who disagreed with Hubbard's plan of transformation were not merely "wrong"; they became The Enemy, and, in Scientology parlance, became "fair game", i.e., targets of unrelenting opposition about which Scientologists should feel no moral qualms. Indeed, within the coterie of new religions Scientology has gained a reputation for its belligerent tendency to practice pre-emptive aggression through lawsuits and quasi-legal harassment. Wallis presents its run-ins with Federal Food and Drug agents and other agencies over use of its "E-Meters", crude polygraphs that allegedly reveal unconscious psychological problems (although he does not include Scientology's more recent difficulties with the Federal Bureau of Investigation which raided Scientology offices and confiscated files, alleging that Scientologists had infiltrated government agencies to learn future plans of surveillance over the movement.) A

sense of this aggressiveness is clear in Wallis' narrative as is the process called "deviance amplification".
In "deviance amplification", a minority movement's fear
of persecution (however paranoid to outsiders) leads
it to take defensive or even offensive steps to protect
itself, which lead larger society to look askance at
it or pressure it, which leads the movement to escalate
its tactics, and so forth.

The theology or doctrine of Scientology is rich
and complex, and neither it nor Wallis' meticulous discussion of its evolution can be briefly summarized and
still do it any justice. Dianetics was preoccupied with
"engrams", or imprinted memory traces, that influence
(for the worse) our performance in daily tasks. The
claim of Dianetics was to explain the origin of engrams
and provide a therapy to "clear" the individual of them.
Later Hubbard infused Scientology with a graduated series
of stages beyond "clear" as well as the concept of a
"thetan" or permanent spiritual essence that survives
through reincarnation. Depending on whom you talk to,
practitioners or critics, Scientology is either bas-
tardized pop psychoanalysis laced with fantasy and
science fiction or a systematic science of personality
reintegration and liberation that works. Along with organizational and doctrinal elaboration, Scientology does
appear to have dropped some of Dianetics' earlier, more
dubious claims, such as the belief that "clears" would
no longer contract head colds or would be immune to bac-
teria and enjoy longevity.

The Road to Total Freedom does provide one rather
unique and valuable feature: Wallis not only permitted
Church of Scientology officials to read his manuscript
before publication and note unnecessary offensive phras-
ings and inaccuracies, but to write an official response
to Wallis' analysis. This response appears as an

appendix, penned by J.C. Simmons, a PhD. in sociology-turned-Scientologist who was formerly on the faculties of the University of Illinois and the University of California at Santa Barbara. Simmons' tone is overtly hostile. He accuses Wallace of bias, sloppy methods, maliciousness, and poor sociological thinking. Simmons is a committed believer who reacts with outrage at the debunking approach of Wallis' treatment of Scientology (though certainly any debunking is secondary to the main purpose of the book). Such phenomena--that is, Wallis' skeptical attitude and Simmons'indignation--are commonplace in sociological research and the responses of minority religions to how they are treated by outside observers. (It is curious that Simmons, himself a pub-lished sociologist, so quickly moved away from this pro-fessional world view once he converted. One would spec-ulate needlessly as to how Simmons would have reacted had Wallis "gone native" [i.e., turned Scientologist himself] and written his account of the movement's de-velopment in glowing terms that hailed Hubbard as a great thinker instead of pointing out Scientology's various internal contradictions and "dirty laundry".) Undoubt-edly much of Simmon's criticism can be attributed to Wallis' irreverent attitude toward Scientology. That reaction is, no doubt, as much an inevitable outcome of all true independent sociological analyses of move-ments with passionate devotees as it is of Wallis' par-ticular orientation.

Wallis' theoretical scheme concerns the cult-to-sect transition discussed earlier in this chapter. His book is unquestionably the major exposition of this model as well as one of the major organizational analyses in modern social movements literature. While the evi-dence clearly reveals the types and extents of various changes made by Hubbard on Dianetics to transform it into Scientology, I am still skeptical that Scientology

is usefully regarded as a sect. Since Scientology never
broke away from anything, it may be more profitably regarded as an advanced cult or a group in the early
church stage--if we do not insist that a "church" re-
semble the universalistic medieval Catholic church.
Hubbard's efforts to reassert authority rescued the
movement from likely extinction and ensured its continuation beyond his own lifetime. When his death does take
place, how Scientology weathers the trauma of problems
of succession, or whether in fact there will be such
problems in the organization, and how Scientology makes
its peace with larger society should reveal more about
the processes described in Wallis' model and the model
of Figure I. It may be that the stage of church is no
longer relevant to social analysis, particularly in modern religiously pluralistic societies where all surviv-
ing cults turn more or less into denominations. In that
case, we may also legitimately ask if we want to call
the institutionalization process sectarianization or
fall back to the already theoretically developed denominationalization.

Second Case

"Moonies" in America:
Cult, Church and Crusade
David G. Bromley and Anson D. Shupe, Jr.

Unlike the reaction of Scientology to Wallis' book,
"Moonies" in America has been generally well received
by its subject, the Unification Church of America. This
is not because sociologists Bromley and Shupe performed
a whitewash. Indeed, the book details the Church's manipulative recruitment and fundraising practices, internal factionalism, and leadership blunders. It relies

in part on information less than freely offered by the movement during the course of thorough congressional investigations damaging to the Church's image. Ultimately the authors conclude that the "Moonies'" idealistic vision of the Kingdom of God on earth is doomed, the movement in classic sectarian fashion fast turning into exactly what it set out to avoid becoming--yet another Christian offshoot, albeit of oriental extraction.

Why then its relatively positive reaction? The answer can be found in two features about how the analysis approached its topic. Contrast <u>"Moonies" in America</u> with the quality and character of other books on the Unification Church. As a genre they are little better than the sorts of tracts of theological refutation that have confronted Mormons, Catholics, and other onetime fringe groups, laced with exaggerated claims of the "Moonies'" mysterious powers to brainwash, self-serving testimonies of prompted exmembers, and ominous warnings of the "Moon threat" to the American way of life that border on sheer hysteria. Compared to what had been written on them previously, a neutral analysis of the Unification Church that did not begin from assumptions that its members were conspiratorial demons or zombies must have seemed refreshing to UC leaders, no matter what else it said.

A second feature of Bromley and Shupe's analysis influencing its positive reception by "Moonies" is the fact that their study was conducted from the perspective of "resource mobilization theory". Resource mobilization is a radically organizational approach, as opposed to the typical social psychological perspective of social movements, that understands the development or demise of social movements in terms of their abilities to obtain and manage certain critical resources, such as members, money, ideology, reputation and publicity. Thus conversion, for example, usually conceptualized solely as a social psychological phenomenon affecting the individual, is conceptualized by Bromley and Shupe as an organizational process: How does the group operate recruitment in order to cast as wide a net as possible? How does it then channel and transform diverse motives for joining so that members internalize movement goals? How can individuals' pursuit of personal spiritual fulfillment become aligned with organizational needs? How does a small deviant movement committed to voluntary (not coercive) change successfully rely on the very society it condemns for support in its drive to change the world? This response mobilization approach, because of its emphasis on structural variables, is thus less burdened with inferences about the mental states of members before or after they join a fringe religion and is unconcerned with speculations about founders' sincerity or motives. (Indeed, it is precisely the possibilities for bias and invalid psychological assumptions discussed earlier in this volume that led many sociologists to take up the resource mobilization perspective.) The "Moonies" may have made plenty of mistakes, may be naive about the very organizational pressures and processes they are experiencing, and on occasion may be more concerned about their goals than the means they use to achieve these, but they are not crazy. Bromley and Shupe regard their movement both as an understandable (certainly not mysterious) wrinkle on the face of American religious change and an interesting vehicle for furthering sociological theory. This is an independent point of view that obviously would have some value to an extremely besieged minority religion.

In a sense this study engages in debunking the entire cult controversy of which the Unification Church was clearly one protagonist. On the one hand it provides detailed information on the movement's historical development, from the original vision of teenage Sun Myung Moon in which Jesus Christ supposedly commissioned Moon to finish the restoration of God's Kingdom on earth and thus fulfill God's providence for mankind, to the Church's early (and bare subsistence) missionary efforts on the west coast in the early 1960s, to its much publicized expansion during the early 1970s and later embroilment in conflict with a coalition of hostile groups and institutions. It reveals the actual decisions, false starts, pragmatic shifts in doctrine, and strategies that brought the Church considerably more notoriety than its size alone warranted (its actual size, despite wild claims reported in the media, probably never topped a modest several thousand members in the United States). On the other hand, it examines the anti-cult movement which arose in opposition to various "cults", of which the Unification Church was simply the most visible. This movement, comprised of regional groups of parents who "lost" their adult children to the "cults" as well as church leaders, became an indispensable part of analyzing the Church's fortunes since some anti-cultists not only lobbied for government intervention to stop "cult" activities but also engaged in vigilante-style abductions of their offspring. The latter practice, in which the families tried to reassert authority over youths whose conversions seemed inexplicable, was premised on the assumption that "cults" brainwash (or program) members and was termed deprogramming. Thus the anti-cultists as well become targets of debunking.

This study ends on a note of fatalism: that the utopian communal model of a family that was the inspiration for the Unificationist movement is fundamentally incompatible with the strategies and structures that develop as the movement expands, hence despite members' best intentions the sect will eventually accommodate and lose its radical nature. This may be true, but Bromley and Shupe, in their concern to utilize the resource mobilization perspective, did not provide clear indications of how or to what extent accomodation will occur. Sociologists have long recognized that people in organizations, no matter how rigid or bureaucratic, engage in patterned evasion of rules, role requirements, and processes that are meant to turn them into ideal members. A view of the Unificationist movement that sees members passively and unquestioningly pursuing orders from above, whether directly from Moon or any other superior, seems unrealistically mechanistic. We are given little evidence of this individual data, i.e., aspirations, skills, and alternative visions. Thus, while the authors analyzed the recruitment and socialization procedures from an organizational perspective, we must wonder about the actual amounts of individual patterned evasion going on within the movement's various operations. Such factors may retard or even alter the course of accommodation. While the "Moonies" will probably never make over the world in the image proclaimed by Rev. Moon, they can shape their sectarian world according to whatever images they want. With only Moon's ambitious statements of what they should achieve and skeptical estimates of what they could achieve, we are left to speculate, in the absence of knowing more about the individuals within the group structure, what they actually will achieve.

NOTES

[1]This point is at times not clearly understood by students or even non-sociologist academics. Actually

the concept of a group as something emergent is fairly straightforward. Sociologists maintain that individuals interacting with one another produce as a group of individuals something that did not exist on the individual level before they came together. Nor can this emergent property of the group be "reduced" or explained adequately in individual (psychological) terms. An analogy would be water: H_2O has distinct physical properties that hydrogen and oxygen separately do not possess. Norms, or shared understandings that are the results of compromise and mutual agreement, are sociologically emergent. The French sociologist Emile Durkheim termed such group-level patterns or phenomena "social facts". An example of a social fact in economics would be inflation. It makes no sense to speak of inflation when you have only one person. To have inflation there must exist at least two persons to exchange goods and services who in turn create a market. A market is not a psychological concept. Inflation is a group-level, not an individual-level, phenomenon (though it certainly has psychological effects). It is real and can be studied in its own right.

[2] It is interesting to contrast Lofland's description of the "Moonies" as part of this general occult milieu researched before the protest movements of the 1960s began, with Bromley and Shupe's analysis of the same group during its period of aggressive expansion as part of a general religious reawakening in the early 1970s following the protest movements of the 1960s (see the Second Case in this chapter). With those upheavals in mind the latter authors were understandably led to interpret the movement's growth in terms of revitalization and dislocation.

[3] Nelson found further support for this point that cult members seek personal psychic or mystical experi-

ence in a later (1972) article dealing with characteristics of members of the cultic Spiritualists National Union in Great Britain. In a sample of 109 persons, 49% reported having experienced some "psychic gift" before joining the Spiritualist movement (27% of the sample experienced such gifts by the age of 16). Another 34% claimed to have developed psychic abilities after entering the movement. An earlier case study of conversion processes in the first missionary unit of the Unification Church during the early 1960s (see Lofland and Stark, 1965) also emphasized the fact that the persons most susceptible to proselytization possessed background with predisposing conditions, among these spiritual restlessness and interest in occult or esoteric religion.

[4] A number of more recent, less classically trained sociologists seem virtually to have abandoned this Marxist-based orientation. It is, for example, virtually useless in explaining largely middle and upper-middle class membership in contemporary groups such as the Unification Church and the Hare Krishna movement.

[5] Even a group as recently arrived as the Unification Church, because of its rapid growth and ambitious involvement in secular affairs, finds itself accomodating in spite of its best intentions. Its utopian visions within the past decade have been gradually moving it toward the status of an established sectarian group. Its millenarian expectations, once a staple of Rev. Moon's early 1970s speeches, are now downplayed (the date for realizing the millennium has been pushed back beyond the year 2000 from its original 1981 deadline) and long-term economic development rather than short-run realization of the Kingdom of God on earth is being emphasized. One only has to examine changing practices in the movement, such as the institutionalization of three-year "engagement periods" before arranged marriage (a necessity to insure marital compatibility as the

group grows and Moon no longer personally knows the personalities of matched couples in the United States) or
something as prosaic as the formation of a collegiate
soccer team at the Unification Theological Seminary (they
beat Army's team in 1979), to see the process at work.
(See Personal Interviews, 1980.)

[6] I have obviously glossed over the particulars of
this process in presenting only the most general summary
of its effects. Niebuhr was not a sociologist but contributed a classic in sociological analysis. For an
accessible, readable summary and critique of his main
theoretical argument, see Wilson (1978:137-68).

REFERENCES

Balch, Robert W. and David Taylor. 1977. "Becoming a
    Sect: A Study of Social Change in a UFO Cult."
    Paper presented at the annual meeting of the Pa-
    cific Sociological Association. Sacramento, CA.

Bromley, David G. and Anson D. Shupe, Jr. 1979. "Moonies"
    in America: Cult, Church and Crusade. Beverly Hills,
    CA: Sage.

Buckner, H. Taylor. 1968. "The Flying Saucerians: An
    Open Door Cult." Pp. 223-30 in Marcello Truzzi,
    ed., Sociology and Everyday Life. Englewood Cliffs,
    NJ: Prentice-Hall.

Clark, Elmer T. 1949. The Small Sects in America.
    Nashville: Abingdon Press.

Demerath, N.J. III and Victor Thiessen. 1966. "On Spitt-
    ing Against the Wind: Organizational Precariousness
    and Irreligion." American Journal of Sociology 71
    (May):674-87.

Durham, G. Homer. 1942. "Administrative Organization
    of the Mormon Church." Political Science Quarterly
    57 (March):51-71.

Eisenstadt, S.N., ed. 1968. Max Weber on Charisma and
    Institution Building. Chicago: University of
    Chicago Press.

Eister, Allan W. 1974. "Culture Crises and New Religious
    Movements: A Paradigmatic Statement of a Theory
    of Cults." Pp. 612-27 in Irving I. Zaretsky and
    Mark P. Leone, eds., Religious Movements in Contem-
    porary America. Princeton, NJ: Princeton University
    Press.

_____. 1972. "An Outline of a Structural The-
    ory of Cults." Journal for the Scientific Study
    of Religion 11 (December):319-33.

_____. 1967. "Toward a Radical Critique of
    Church-Sect Typologizing: Comment on 'Some Critical
    Observations on the Church-Sect Dimension.'" Journal
    for the Scientific Study of Religion 16 (April):
    85-90.

Fauset, Arthur H. 1970. Black Gods of the Metropolis.
    New York: Octagon Books.

Foss, Daniel A. and R.W. Larkin. 1979. "The Roar of the
    Lemming: Youth, Post-Movement Groups, and the Life
    Construction Crisis." Pp. 264-85 in Harry M. Johnson,
    ed., Religious Change and Continuity. San Francisco:
    Josey-Bass.

Glock, Charles Y. and Robert N. Bellah, eds. 1976. The
    New Religious Consciousness. Berkeley, CA: Univer-
    sity of California Press.

Goode, Erich. 1967a. "Some Critical Observations on the
    Church-Sect Dimension." Journal for the Scientific
    Study of Religion 6 (April):69-77.

_____. 1967b. "Further Reflections on the Church-Sect Typology." Journal for the Scientific Study of Religion 6 (April):270-75.

Greeley, Andrew M. 1972. The Denominational Society. Glenview, IL: Scott, Foresman and Company.

Gustafson, Paul. 1967. "UO-US-PS-PO: A Restatement of Troeltsch's Church-Sect Typology." Journal for the Scientific Study of Religion 6 (April):64-8.

Hargrove, Barbara. 1979. The Sociology of Religion. Arlington Heights, IL: AMH.

Harris, Sara. 1971. Father Divine. (Revised Edition) New York: Macmillian.

Harrison, Paul M. 1971. Authority and Power in the Free Church Tradition. Carbondale, IL: Southern Illinois University Press.

Heckethorn, Charles William. 1965. The Secret Societies of All Ages and Countries. Vol I. New York: University Books.

Hughes, Philip. 1949. A History of the Church. Vol. I. New York: Sheed and Ward.

Johnson, Benton. 1971. "Church and Sect Revisited." Journal for the Scientific Study of Religion 10 (Summer):124-37.

_____. 1963. "On Church and Sect." American Sociological Review 22 (May):539-49.

_____. 1957. "A Critical Appraisal of Church-Sect Typology." American Sociological Review 22 (February):89-92.

Kallen, Horace M. 1951. "Cults." Pp. 618-21 in Edwin R. Saligman, ed. Encyclopedia of the Social Sciences. Vol. 4. New York: Macmillan.

Latourette, Kenneth S. 1937. Expansion of Christianity. Vol. I: The First Five Centuries. (Fourth Edition) new York: Harper.

Leone, Mark P. 1974. "The Economic Basis for the Evolu-
    tion of Mormon Religion." Pp. 722-66 in Irving I.
    Zaretsky and Mark P. Leone, eds., Religious Move-
    ments in Contemporary America. Princeton, NJ:
    Princeton University Press.

_____ and Rodney Stark. 1965. "Becoming a World-
    Saver: A Theory of Conversion to a Deviant Perspec-
    tive." American Sociological Review 30 (December):
    862-74.

Lofland, John. 1966. Doomsday Cult. Englewood Cliffs,
    NJ: Prentice-Hall.

Nelson, Geoffrey K. 1972. "The Membership of a Cult:
    The Spiritualists National Union." Review of Re-
    ligious Research 13 (Spring):170-77.

_____. 1960. "The Spiritualist Movement
    and the Need for a Redefinition of Cult." Journal
    for the Scientific Study of Religion 8 (Spring):
    153-60.

Niebuhr, H. Richard. 1929. The Social Sources of Denom-
    inationalism. New York: Henry Holt & Co.

O'Dea, Thomas F. 1966. The Sociology of Religion. Engle-
    wood Cliffs, NJ: Prentice-Hall.

Pilarzyk, Thomas. 1978. "The Origin, Development, and
    Decline of a Youth Culture Religion: An Application
    of Sectarianization Theory." Review of Religious
    Research 20 (Fall):23-43.

Richardson, James T. 1979. "From Cult to Sect: Creative
    Eclecticism in New Religious Movements." Pacific
    Sociological Review 22 (April):139-66.

_____, Mary W. Stewart, and Robert B.
    Simmonds. 1979. Organized Miracles: A Study of a
    Contemporary, Youth, Communal, Fundamentalist Or-
    ganization. New Brunswick, NJ: Transaction Press.

Robbins, Thomas, Dick Anthony, M. Doucas and T. Curtis.
    1976. "The Last Civil Religion: Reverend Moon and

the Unification Church." Sociological Analysis 37 (Summer):111-25.

Robinson, John. 1974. "A Song, A Shout, and A Prayer." Pp. 212-35 in C. Eric Lincoln, ed., The Black Experience in Religion. Garden City, NY: Doubleday Anchor.

Shupe, Jr., Anson D. 1981. "The Guardians: Anti-Organizational Fetishism in a Mail-Order Cult." Forthcoming in Ray B. Browne, ed., Fetishes and Fetishism in American Society. Bowling Green, OH: Popular Press.

_____. 1976. "Disembodied Access" and Technological Constraints on Organizational Developments: A Study of Mail-Order Religions." Journal for the Scientific Study of Religion 15 (June):177-85.

Simmel, Georg. 1950. The Sociology of Georg Simmel. Trans. and ed. by Kurt H. Wolff. New York: The Free Press.

Stark, Werner. 1967. The Sociology of Religion. Vol. Two: Sectarian Religion. New York: Fordham University Press.

Theissen, Gerd. 1978. Sociology of Early Palestine Christianity. Trans. by John Bowden. Philadelphia: Fortress Press.

Tiryakian, Edward A. 1972. "Toward the Sociology of Esoteric Culture." American Journal of Sociology 78 (November):491-512.

Troletsch, Ernst. 1960. The Social Teaching of the Christian Churches. Trans. by Olive Wyon. New York: Harper & Row.

Wach, Joachim. 1972. Types of Religious Experience: Christian and Non-Christian. Chicago: University of Chicago Press.

_____. 1967. Sociology of Religion. Chicago:
    University of Chicago Press.

Wallis, Roy. 1977. The Road to Total Freedom. A Soci-
    ological Analysis of Scientology. New York:
    Columbia University Press.

_____. 1974. "Ideology, Authority, and the De-
    velopment of Cultic Movement." Social Research 41
    (Summer):299-327.

Washington, Jr., Joseph R. 1973. Black Sects and Cults.
    Garden City, NY: Doubleday Anchor.

Weber, Max. 1964. The Theory of Social and Economic Or-
    ganization. Trans. by A.M. Henderson and Talcott
    Parsons. Glencoe, IL: The Free Press.

Williston, Walker. 1970. A History of the Christian
    Church. (Third Edition, Revised by R.T. Handy) New
    York: Charles Scribner's Sons.

Wilson, Bryan R. 1959. "An Analysis of Sect Develop-
    ment." American Sociological Review 24 (February):
    3-15.

Wilson, John. 1978. Religion in American Society. The
    Effective Presence. Englewood Cliffs, NJ: Prentice-
    Hall.

_____. 1974. "The Historical Study of Marginal
    American Religious Movements." Pp. 596-611 in
    Irving I. Zaretsky and Mark P. Leone, eds., Re-
    ligious Movements in Contemporary America.
    Princeton, NJ: Princeton University Press.

Wood, James R. 1970. "Authority and Controversial Pol-
    icy: The Churches and Civil Rights." American Soci-
    ological Review 35 (December):1057-69.

Wuthnow, Robert. 1978. Experimentation in American Re-
    ligion. Berkeley, CA: University of California
    Press.

SUGGESTED FURTHER READING

Brannen, Noah S. 1968. Soka Gakkai, Japan's Militant Buddhists. Richmond, VA: John Knox Press.

Bellah, Robert N. 1968. "Civil Religion in America." Pp. 3-23 in William G. McLoughlin and Robert N. Bellah, eds., Religion in America. Boston: Beacon Press.

Gerlach, Luther P. and Virginia Hine. 1968. "Five Factors Crucial to the Growth and Spread of a Modern Religious Movement." Journal for the Scientific Study of Religion 7 (Spring):23-40.

Greeley, Andrew M. 1972. Unsecular Man. New York: Schocken Books.

Hennan, Edward F. 1973. Mystery, Magic, and Miracle: Religion in a Post-Aquarian Age. Englewood Cliffs, NJ: Prentice-Hall.

Murver, Vatro. 1975. "Toward a Sociological Theory of Religious Movements." Journal for the Scientific Study of Religion 14 (September):229-56.

Norbeck, Edward. 1970. Religion and Society in Modern Japan: Continuity and Change. Houston, TX: Tourmaline Press.

O'Dea, Thomas F. 1954. "Mormonism and the Avoidance of Sectarian Stagnation: A Study of Church, Sect, and Incipient Nationality." American Journal of Sociology 60 (November):285-93.

Stephan, Karen and G. Edward Stephan. 1973. "Religion and the Survival of Utopian Communities." Journal for the Scientific Study of Religion 12 (March): 89-100.

Weber, Max. 1963. The Sociology of Religion. Trans. by Ephraim Fischoff. Boston: Beacon Press.

Wilson, Bryan. 1961. Sects and Society. London: Heineman.

SOME THOUGHTS FOR FURTHER CONSIDERATION

It should be apparent to readers that the social structure approach to studying fringe religions dispenses with the motives of founders, psychological states of members, and the truth foundations of beliefs: all elements of a religious group that other perspectives, as well as the average person on the street, find important. Its narrow focus permits a sociologist to trace a group's activities and offices over time as if these were painted on a sort of longitudinal wall mural. More than other approaches, it could even serve as "feedback" to an enlightened cult or sect leader on how to anticipate and perhaps avoid organizational pitfalls as the group grows.

But at what point(s) do nonempirical religious "truth" and sociological "fatalism" interface? Can they ever be reconciled without one "reducing", explaining away, or threatening the validity of the other?

THE HISTORICAL PERSPECTIVE

Historians do not simply tally the trivia of the
past, like ants building a mound, until the outline of
what occurred before the present becomes self-evident.
They exhume details, it is true, but they do so in order
to trace the continuities of specific events and developments with antecedent conditions. The historians' job
is thus not simply to uncover what once happened but
rather to construct a context of meaning for what happened. The result is, of course, their meaning--the historians' meaning, that is--and not necessarily the meaning of events for the persons who lived them. Indeed,
it is a larger meaning than those historical actors
could ever have constructed, pieced together from
knowledge of later and earlier events, that helps sift
significance from insignificance and place events in
some relation of importance to one another.

There have been far too many studies by historians
for me even to attempt here a comprehensive overview
of their interpretations and approaches to new religions. Analysis of the sheer mass of monographs on religious movements, cults and sects published in the English language alone would be an awesome task. Therefore,
this chapter will depend more than previous ones on
a contrast between two classic documents, both of which
were concerned with the conflict surrounding a fringe
religion on American soil over 150 years ago. I want
to focus narrowly on the anti-Catholic nativistic controversy of pre-civil war New England. It may seem

odd to some modern readers to speak of the mainline
Roman Catholic church as a fringe religious group, but
in early nineteenth century America it was just that.
Catholics were considered by the Protestant majority
to be deviant, foreign, sinister, and immoral, and because of this perception they became the targets of legal and illegal discrimination. I believe that the conflict surrounding the right of the Catholic church even
to exist in this country at one time will provide a useful illustration of how a later professional historian's broader approach to "making sense" of it all dif-
fers greatly from that of a partisan person contemporary
to the conflict. It may also lend the modern controversy over religious "cults" some long-range perspective.[1]

THE IRISH CATHOLICS AND NATIVISTIC BACKLASH

The Irish Catholics of the early nineteenth century
were the first Caucasian Europeans to challenge seriously the Anglo-Saxon ideology of assimilation into American society: that all immigrants could and should blend
with the dominant Anglo-Saxon Protestant (British) majority culture first implanted in the eastern seaboard
colonies. Their most obvious unblendable characteristic
was their Catholicism. Indeed, they clung fiercely to
it as an important source of ethnic identity and unity,
and persecution of them on Catholicism's behalf only
strengthened their resolve to resist complete assimilation.

The Irish came in different decades for different
but related reasons. In the 1820s and 1830s Ireland
experienced severe over-population and English political
maneuvers that left many farmers landless and penniless.

In the mid-1840s there occurred several widespread potato famines which further threw larger numbers of persons into desperate straits. England was only too happy to export Irish by the tens of thousands. Many went to Canada, and many of these migrated south into the United States. Many others came to the country directly, tending to cluster in the New England States, particularly in New York and Massachusetts among other places. Marty (1970:128) estimates that whereas in 1816 there were only 6000 Irish in the United States, by 1850 there were almost one million.

In order to understand the hostile reaction against the Irish which gradually mounted throughout the first half of the century, two factors need to be kept in mind:

The first factor was the obvious religious one. Anglo-Saxon Protestants carried over into the nineteenth century a legacy of distrust and illwill toward Catholicism begun centuries earlier with the Protestant Reformation. In the British experience in particular, England had once fought (and won) a desperate war with Imperial Catholic Spain (sinking the latter's Armada in the English Channel) and during Elizabethan times enacted discriminatory anti-Catholic laws. As Billington (1974:10) notes: "It was this background of bigotry and hatred that was transferred from the old world to the new." The French and Indian War (Protestant British versus Catholic French) in the mid-eighteenth century exacerbated anti-Catholic feelings. In the years 1776-78, for instance, the states of New Jersey, Georgia, New York, Vermont, and both North and South Carolina included clauses in their state constitutions that barred Catholics from holding state office (Billington 1974:37).

The second factor important to consider was the economic threat posed by cheap Irish labor. Particularly in the New England cities of the 1800s they threatened

to compete for the jobs of the unskilled and semi-skilled
working classes. Says historian Carl Wittke (1970:117):

> Native Americans resented the competition of
> Irish laborers and accused the British of de-
> liberately dumping "the poor, the vicious and
> the degraded" upon the United States. Still
> others believed the Jesuits and the Church
> were encouraging Catholic paupers to immigrate
> in order to undermine the economic foundations
> of the nation.

Likewise, Shannon (1966:141) locates much of the later
persecution fundamentally in the economics of labor competition.   According to him, the religious factor was
only a pretext for repressing the Irish. Shannon concludes: "The Irish working man in the next block and
not the Pope in Rome was the real enemy."

The nativistic (xenophobic and jingoistic would
also be suitable adjectives) reaction which emerged in
the first half of the nineteenth century fed off these
two concerns: the religious and the economic. They became fused into a rationalization of political fear.
This fear was that Catholics held ultimate allegiance
to the Pope in Rome ("popery" became synonymous with
Catholicism), and if sufficient numbers of Irish could
form a Catholic voting bloc, then the political sovereignty of the (Protestant) United States would be soon-
after subverted.[2] Historian Olson (1979:80-1) reports:

> In New England especially, many Americans
> thought the Irish threatened Anglo-Saxon civ-
> ilization.   Irish immigration coincided with
> the democratic, anti-authoritarian worship
> of the common man popular during the era of
> President Andrew Jackson, and Roman Catholi-
> cism seemed contradictory because it gave
> authoritarian power to the pope. Some Yankees

questioned Irish allegiance, doubting that
they could become "true Americans" because
dual loyalty to a religious monarchy and a
liberal democracy seemed impossible . . . .
With their devotion to the liberation of the
old country Northern Ireland, their religion,
and their communities, they defied Anglo-
American conformity. Many Americans resented
such pride.

Similarly, Marty (1970:128) comments:

Catholicism was always represented as a political religion which had its designs of world
subjugation through coercive means . . . .
The Catholic immigrant was often pictured as
a person of low morals and bad habits, racially inferior, congenitally alien, and histor-
ically unable to understand or contribute to
a free society.

A good example of such sentiments can be found in
the writings of Samuel F. B. Morse, a painter and the
inventor of the telegraph who became an active anti-
Catholic spokesman. In one essay printed in 1835 (reprinted in Morse, 1968:158-9) he wrote:

It is a fact that popery is opposed in its
very nature to democratic republicanism; and
it is, therefore, as a political system, as
well as religious, opposed to civil and religious liberty, and consequently to our form
of government.

Morse was convinced of a foreign conspiracy to spread
Catholicism throughout the United States:

It is a fact that the agents of these foreign
despots are, for the most part, Jesuits. It
is a fact that the effects of this society

are already apparent in the otherwise unacceptable increase of Roman Catholic cathedrals,
churches, colleges, convents, nunneries, etc.,
in every part of the country; in the sudden
increase of Catholic emigration; in the in-
creased clannishness of the Roman Catholics,
and the boldness with which their leaders are
experimenting on the character of the American
people.

Morse's solution was two-fold: relocation of Catholics
presently in this country to specific restricted areas
for permanent settlement, and immediate immigration/
naturalization laws to deny any future (Catholic) foreign immigrants the right of suffrage.

Morse's sentiments were echoed in numerous sermons,
pamphlets and newspaper editorials, in anti-Irish jokes
(similar to the ethnic jokes that mock Polish-Americans,
Mexican-Americans, and other minorities), and in the
speeches of nativisitic speakers. One such speaker,
Edmond A. Freeman, a rabble-rouser who made the rounds
of lecture circuits in the 1880s when anti-Irish feelings had not disappeared, delivered a remarkable double
ethnic/racial slur when he claimed that "the best remedy
for whatever is amiss in America would be if every Irishman should kill a negro and be hanged for it." (Gossett,
1965:109)

Thus a stereotypical folklore that passed for fact
grew up around Irish Roman Catholics, and it was as likely to be passed on from the pulpit as propagated by
newspapers. "There was a growing belief in the minds
of Americans at the time that all these impoverished
aliens were not able to care for themselves and never
had been; that America was being used as a dumping
ground for destitute Europeans." (Billington, 1974:58)
Historian David Brion Davis (1960), in comparing the

similar mythologies developed around Free Masons, Mormons and Roman Catholics, cites the latter group as being accused of incest, brutality and sadism, idolatry, and infanticide. Davis is of the opinion that in many cases the puritanical Protestants of New England projected in psychoanalytic fashion their own socially unacceptable fantasies, their own moral confusion caused by a burgeoning, industrializing, pluralistic culture, and their own guilt onto the unfortunate Catholic scapegoats. Nunneries, behind whose walls Victorian Protestants imagined all manner of sexual perversions taking place in lieu of the prescribed celibacy, offered perfect targets for such projections. Comments Davis:

> If the conscience of many Americans were troubled by the growth of red light districts in major cities, they could divert their attention to the "legalized brothels" called nunneries, for which no one was responsible but lecherous Catholic priests . . . . The literature of countersubversion could thus serve the double purpose of vicariously fulfilling repressed desires, and of releasing the tension and guilt arising from rapid social change and conflicting social values. (1960:220)

APOSTATES AND NATIVISM

Early in the century anti-Catholic literature had made its appearance. In 1812, for example, Anthony Gavin published A Master Key to Popery, Giving a Full Account of All the Customs of the Priests and Friars and the Rites and Ceremonies of the Popish Religion, and in 1821 Jeremiah Odd published a book in Vermont entitled Popery

Unveiled (see Billington, 1974:92-8), both "shocking exposés." However, the anti-Catholic movement awaited the inevitable appearance of apostates (defectors) and alleged (pseudo) apostates to provide the real fuel for public repression. Apostates have a special value for countermovements.[3] They alone can provide what elsewhere David Bromley and I (see Shupe and Bromley), 1980:154) have referred to as "smoking gun" evidence against a group. While opponents may suspect the worst of a group, they can only relate what they at best know secondhand. Apostates, however, can claim to have seen firsthand and often personally participated in various horrors. Their testimony is that of the insider and as such provides an apparently irrefutable confirmation for the propaganda of a group's opponents. In sociological terms apostasy is a particular status, and one who assumes it--or can make others believe that one is an actual apostate--gains a great deal of credibility. The appearance of persons claiming to have been members of some unpopular group and now willing to expose it is well-nigh inevitable in such conflicts over social movements, for just as the movement or group in question (in this case the Catholics) tries to refute opponents' allegations, so the latter "anti's" feel under greater pressure to come up with the better "proof" for their claims. Who can provide better proof of misdeeds than a confessed former perpetrator of them? In the following examples of apostates' testimonies we can see this pressure to produce sensational evidence vividly displayed. In most cases none of the persons claiming to be apostates of Catholicism had ever really been Catholics. Their "confessions" were actually fabricated propaganda. However, the anti-Catholic movement's need to produce apostates (an inevitability from a sociological viewpoint) gave rise to their manufacture.

In the mid-1830s, when the "Catholic issue" had become extremely volatile for the reasons discussed earlier, there appeared a parade of apostates and their published testimonies purporting to offer shocking revelations of life in convents, e.g., the sexual exploitation of young nuns by priests, frequent orgies, aborted fetuses resulting from sexual promiscuity, and so forth. One apostate who never even published any revelations but whose temporary defection served to fire peoples' imaginations was Elizabeth Harrison. A legitimate Ursuline nun and teacher with apparent emotional problems, she abruptly left her convent in Charlestown, Massachusetts in late July, 1834 and fled to the home of several of her pupils. Though she was returned to the convent (embarrassed, repentant, and at her own request), local newspapers and ministers picked up and spread the rumors that she had originally escaped the "dungeon" in the convent basement and been forcibly "kidnapped" by the Catholic bishop's agents. Despite attempts by the convent to dispel the rumors of Elizabeth Harrison's supposed confession of life inside the convent, tensions mounted and the mood of Protestants in Charlestown grew more hostile. Billington (1974:161) quotes one placard circulated publically:

> Go ahead! To arms! To arms! Ye brave and
> free the avenging sword unsheath! Leave not
> one stone upon another of that curst nunnery
> that prostitutes female virtue and liberty
> under the garb of Holy Religion. When Bonaparte
> opened the Nunneries of Europe he found cords
> of infants skulls.

On August 11, 1834, after such promptings, an incensed mob of 1000 men drove the occupants out and burned the Ursuline convent to the ground (while much of the town watched).

In the next several years there was an epidemic of "refugee" Catholics willing to "tell all" about the Church to eager Protestant listeners. The same year of the convent's burning Samuel B. Smith, a self-proclaimed ex-priest, published The Downfall of Babylon, or The Triumph of Truth Over Popery (see Billington, 1974:203-4). In 1835 Rebecca Reed, who claimed to be an escaped nun (she had never actually been admitted to a convent, having been dismissed as unqualified after four months of the required six-month probationary period), published one of the all-time bestselling potboilers, the ghostwritten Six Months in a Convent. It provided detailed descriptions of exploitive convent life complete with anecdotes of how nuns were systematically degraded, subjected to sadistic violence, and kept malnourished. That same year, Billington (1974:193) reports, a published sequel appeared in Boston bookstores, entitled: A Supplement to Six Months in a Convent, Confirming the Narrative of Rebecca Therese Read, by the Testimony of More Than 100 Witnesses.

The next year appeared an even bigger bestseller, Maria Monk's Awful Disclosures of the Hotel Dieu Convent of Montreal, or the Secrets of Black Nunnery Revealed (another 1836 edition carried the slightly different title: Awful Disclosures by Maria Monk of the Hotel Dieu Nunnery of Montreal). I will discuss Maria Monk and her book as the First Case later in this chapter. Here I note only that she, like Rebecca Read, was a bogus apostate, having never actually been a nun but rather (in Monk's case) an inmate in an insane asylum run by nuns. She became pregnant by an outspoken anti-Catholic minister, and it appears that the two (or more) of them concocted her "testimony" so as to further the cause of anti-Catholicism, come up with an acceptable explanation for her pregnancy out of wedlock (she claimed she was raped by a priest), and make a good deal of money

in the process. (The book accomplished all three purposes for a time.) The book provided the most extreme
examples of the anti-Catholic stories. For instance,
Monk claimed to have witnessed perversions galore: ex-
ecutions, abortions. infanticides, and sexual orgies.
The Catholics were appalled by the book and published
that same year their own refutation, entitled Awful Exposure of the Atrocious Plot formed by Certain Individuals Against the Clergy and Nuns of Lower Canada: Through
the Intervention of Maria Monk, which argued that Maria
Monk was an imposter. Almost immediately, however,
Samuel B. Smith, the "renegade priest" mentioned earlier,
reappeared to respond with Decisive Confirmation of the
Awful Disclosure of Maria Monk, Proving Her Residence
in the Hotel Dieu Nunnery and the Existence of Subterranean Passages. Smith further complicated the situation and added seeming confirmation to Monk's claims
by almost simultaneously publishing the case of another
"escaped nun," Sister Francis Patrick, in The Escape
of Sister Francis Patrick: Another Nun from the Hotel
Dieu Nunnery of Montreal. Francis Patrick claimed to
have known Maria Monk in the convent and became a brief
cause celebre in her own right. Finally, the following
year Maria Monk published her own sequel, Further Disclosures of Maria Monk, Concerning the Hotel Dieu Nunnery of Montreal. In the meantime, otherwise sane and
responsible persons were accepting these "revelations"
as truth and calling for "something to be done" about
these alleged Catholic abominations (recall the Morse
quote earlier in this chapter).

    This, then, was the background of the anti-Catholic
controversy of early-to-mid nineteenth century America
against which the two case studies to follow can be understood. It was an era in which Protestants' paranoia
of Roman Catholic theocratic conspiracies was indulged

to extremes both by sincere men and women and by fast-buck opportunists. It is but one example for the cynical to use in challenging the myth that America has always been the land of religious refuge and tolerance. From a historical perspective it suggests the proposition that religious pluralism in this country evolved as much (or more) because of the reluctant but pragmatic realization that no one group could subjugate the others and not because tolerance flowed automatically out of constitutional traditions.

From a sociological perspective informed by history, it further suggests the generalization I made earlier: that anti-movements seeking to repress certain groups eagerly recruit apostates who will piously recount their exploitation and thus provide evidence, however embellished and exaggerated, that repression is justified. Failing to recruit such persons, they will manufacture them out of little more than imagination guided by prejudice. The anti-Catholic movement is instructive about this apostasy process, but it is hardly unique. As Oliver (1980) has shown, apostates and their horrorific testimonies play essentially the same "smoking gun" role in a variety of anti-movements, both religious and secular. For example, anti-Mormonism in the nineteenth century witnessed Female Life Among the Mormons: A Narrative of Many Years' Personal Experience, By the Wife of a Mormon Elder Recently Returned from Utah (Ward, 1857), Fifteen Years Among the Mormons: Being the Narrative of Mrs. Mary Ettie Smith (Green, 1857), and Wife No. 19: or The Story of a Life in Bondage, Being a Complete Exposé of Mormonism (Young, 1875). Hopkins (1830) produced a similar contribution to this genre with Renunciation of Free Masonry. Recently the controversy over new religions has stimulated the reappearance of the same predictable wave of publications

by persons seeking lucrative royalties and/or justifica-
tion for their own involvement in fringe religious groups
which they now reject. Jeannie Mills (1979) and Bonnie
Thielmann (1979), apostates of Jim Jones' People's
Temple, respectively penned Six Years with God and The
Broken God. Rachel Martin (1979) apologized for her
exploits as a member of the Garbage Eaters in Escape.
The controversial Unification Church of Sun Myung Moon
has, not surprisingly, produced its share of disgruntled
ex-members (some deprogrammed, some not) willing to
share their unpleasant experiences with the public and
lend their testimonies to forward the goals of the current anti-cult movement: see, for example, Crazy for
God (Edwards, 1979), Hostage to Heaven (Underwood and
Underwood, 1979), and Moonstruck (Wood and Vitek, 1979).

   This feature of historical analyses--that historians seek the broader meaning of specific events with
as much dispassion as they can maintain--is one little
pleasing to the prejudices and short-run perspectives
of individuals caught up in the personal tragedies,
fears and ambiguities surrounding new religions. No
one likes to see his or her memoirs, feelings or beliefs
reduced to being considered merely part of a genre or
type of literature, least of all those persons who may
have legitimately belonged to a fringe religious group
and now sincerely believe they were duped or exploited.
Despite their protests, however, historians must labor
to construct a larger, sometimes recurrent meaning out
of many discrete events and issues that for the actors
involved seem unique and extraordinary.

CASE STUDIES

First Case

<u>Awful</u> <u>Disclosures</u> <u>of</u> <u>the</u>
<u>Hotel</u> <u>Dieu</u> <u>Convent</u> <u>of</u> <u>Montreal</u>,
<u>or</u> <u>The</u> <u>Secrets</u> <u>of</u> <u>the</u> <u>Black</u> <u>Nunnery</u> <u>Revealed</u>
Maria Monk

Pseudo-apostate Maria Monk's ghostwritten testimonial <u>Awful</u> <u>Disclosures</u> was a shocker, even for Protestant audiences familiar with the standard litany of anti-Catholic allegations in the 1800s. The book went through a number of editions and made a good deal of money, continuing to sell long after even Maria Monk herself had been discredited. It is a good example of the independence from reality which propaganda can assume and illustrates the hoary sociological maxim: "What is perceived as real <u>is</u> in its consequences."

Briefly, Maria's testimony told the following horror story: Born of Protestant parents, she had been sent to parochial school in Montreal (not an unusual practice in that era) where she eventually converted and then entered the Hotel Dieu convent. There she was indoctrinated into a paramilitaristic order of sadists and sex maniacs who covered their tracks well by enforcing brutal discipline and sheer degradation on the nuns. For example, Maria recalled the "most disgusting penance" of having to drink the water with which the Mother Superior washed her feet. She reported in sickening detail the execution of one unfortunate nun:

> On the bed the prisoner was laid with her face
> upward, and then bound with cords, so that
> she could not move. In an instant another
> bed was thrown upon her. One of the priests

named Bonin, sprung like a fury first upon
it and stomped upon it, with all his force.
He was speedily followed by the nuns, until
there were as many upon the bed as could find
room and all did what they could, not only
to smother, but to bruise her. Some stood
up and jumped upon the poor girl with their
feet, some with their knees, and others in
different ways seemed to seek how they might
best beat the breath out of her body, and man-
gle it, without coming in direct contact with
it or seeing the effects of their violence....
After a lapse of 15 or 20 minutes, and when
it was presumed that the sufferer had been
smothered, and crushed to death, Father Bonin
and the nuns ceased to trample upon her, and
stepped from the bed. All was motionless and
and silent beneath it.... They then began
to laugh at such inhuman thoughts as occurred
to some of them, rallying each other in the
most unfeeling manner. (116)

Sexual promiscuity was rampant, according to Maria,
and as a new nun she was pointedly instructed by the
Mother Superior that it was her duty to obey every command of the priests, even "criminal intercourse." Indeed
a maze of subterranean corridors supposedly connected
the convent to priests' quarters elsewhere in the area
to facilitate "visitations." At one point Maria was
apparently sadistically treated, raped, and "passed
around" by several priests:

In a private apartment, he treated me in a
brutal manner; and from two other priests,
I afterward received similar usage that eve-
ning. Father Dufrene afterward appeared again;

and I was compelled to remain in company with him until morning. (62)

A number of the "atrocities" which she reported seem remarkably like those leveled at the Unification Church, the Hare Krishnas and other contemporary "cults" by angry ex-members in the media. For example, Maria claims she was continually undernourished and made the victim of psychological coercion (currently referred to by modern anti-cultists as "mind control"):

> For a nun to doubt that she was doing her duty in fulfilling her vows and oaths, was a heinous offense, and we were exhorted always to suppress our doubts, to confess them without reserve, and cheerfully to submit to severe penances on account of them, as the only means of mortifying our evil dispositions, and resisting the temptations of the devil. Thus we learnt in a good degree to resist our minds and consciences, when we felt the first rising of a question about the duty of doing anything required of us. (17)

Perhaps readers now have a sense for the flavor of Maria Monk's "revelations." The most gruesome anecdote was Maria's recounting of the fate of infants born to nuns as a result of fornication with priests. She claimed to witness the matter-of-fact murder of two infants: a priest first baptized them with oil, then an elderly nun callously suffocated them and threw the tiny bodies into a pit in the basement where they were covered with a layer of lime to aid in decomposition. (174) Eventually herself pregnant by a priest and (needless to say) disillusioned by all she had seen, Maria decided to flee and save her own life as well as the child's.

Over a century later it is possible to examine Maria Monk's claims more objectively than perhaps could impassioned, outraged New Englanders in the 1830s. We know not that Maria Monk never wrote Awful Disclosures, and undoubtedly the stories in her testimony tell us more about the people who made them up than about life in the Hotel Dieu convent. As Billington (1974:227ff) has summarized from patient detective work, Maria Monk never spent any time in the Hotel Dieu convent as a nun. Her exposure to convent life and the behavior of nuns came exclusively from her school days and a later period of stay in an insane asylum run by the Catholic Church (this according to her mother's testimony). A committee of outraged Protestants, including clergymen, who went to the real Hotel Dieu convent found that the building in no way resembled Maria's description (no lime pit, no subterranean corridors). Maria and her nativistic supporters replied to this announcement that the Catholics had hastily remodeled the place to hide any evidence that would support her original description, produced other "witnesses" to confirm her story, and blanketly stood by the accuracy of her book. That same year a second "escaped nun" appeared--Sister Francis Patrick, allegedly also of the Hotel Dieu convent--and claimed not only to have known Maria at Montreal but also to have been in on the deception of the Protestant investigatory committee.

Awful Disclosures was most likely written by the real father of Maria's child, a notorious nativist writer and clergyman named William Hoyt. Awful Disclosures no doubt seemed at the time a perfect way out of their delicate dilemma: Maria and child had a believable explanation for her pregnancy out of wedlock as well as royalties from the book on which to live. (Rebecca Reed's Six Months in a Convent published the year before had successfully tested the waters in terms of market appeal.) Far from being ostracized by a society normally holding rigid Victorian scruples about extramarital sex, Maria became a martyr. Moreover, Hoyt had contacts within the leadership of the anti-Catholic movement (which accounts for the confirmatory "evidence" marshalled so spontaneously by sympathetic writers such as the indefatigable Samuel B. Smith). However, things began to go sour not long after the publication of Awful Disclosures. In 1838, Maria bore her second child out of wedlock (no Catholic priest to blame this time), and in an embarassing set of lawsuits in which she claimed Hoyt and various associates had cheated her out of royalities, it emerged that she played little part in authoring either Awful Disclosures or its sequel Further Disclosures published the following year. Her credibility swiftly eroded, and her career as an apostate collapsed. Billington (1936-7) reports that she died in prison convicted of picking pockets.

It should be apparent that with a book such as Maria Monk's the primary historical value lies not in the alleged accuracy or integrity of what it contains but rather in its effects. Billington concludes:

> Maria Monk had played her part: She had demonstrated the profits that could come from anti-Catholic propaganda, especially if it smacked of the pornographic. Much of the credit for the wave of nativism which followed can be attributed to the widely read and accepted Awful Disclosures. (1974:245)

Thus the historian asks what meaning the part lends to the whole, or more specifically, what can we learn of the anti-Catholic movement from this type of book? What were its real effects (or as sociologists would say, what were its functions)? The trick in discerning these broad effects is to possess disciplined logic and rules of evidence--the marks of the trained historian-- and thus it is not a trick, or art, at all. The task requires systematic procedure, and for a brief discussion of the latter I turn to the Second Case.

Second Case

The Origins of Nativism in the United States, 1800-1844
Ray Allen Billington

Billington's Origins of Nativism was originally his doctoral thesis in history presented to Harvard University. It has since been reprinted by Arno Press (a publishing house which specializes in reprinting documents of historical significance; they also reprinted Maria Monk's Awful Disclosures and Rebecca Reed's Six Months in a Convent) and overlaps with Billington's other major work (1952) on the subject. Origins of Nativism is one of the basic reference works on the subject of nativism in the nineteenth century, a classic of thorough historical investigation that relies on the primary sources of its subject matter (for example, original newspaper articles, personal diaries, handbills, and so forth) rather than on the interpretations of other historians. In many places Billington's work has the appearance of a debunking exercise, such as when he examines evidence that Maria Monk did or did not write Awful Disclosures. Such an impression would be mistaken, however. Historical investigation only becomes debunking when it deals with sham and fraud (of which there seems to have been a fair amount in the nativist movement), but that is not its primary intent.

Billington has two main interests in his study. The first is to pursue the origins of nativism beyond its immediate causes in immigration and economic conflict in New England, to understand its more general place in American history instead of merely regarding nativism as something that happened in nineteenth century New England. This he does by tracing the Protestant nature of American culture and its accompanying hostility to Catholicism beginning with the Protestant Reformation and Martin Luther through Tudor England and the colonial settlement of this country. Seen through this broader time perspective, the nineteenth century nativist movement emerges as a particularly virulent outbreak of a religious bigotry that has existed in North America since its earliest settlement by Europeans, not unique but part of a pattern. Billington's study in turn lays the groundwork for understanding the more widespread anti-Immigration and racist movements that took hold of America--not merely laborers and ministers but also intellectuals and the highest officials--later in the same century.

Billington's second interest is to explain the mechanisms of nativism. For example, aside from basic religious hatred and economic insecurity, New England Protestants in the 1830s had further conflict with Catholics over the temperance issue. The average Irishman's attitude toward consumption of alcohol was considerably more lax than the sentiments of the descendents of the Puritans and Congregationalists. Given such background conditions, the occurrence of a precipitating factor such as Awful Disclosures to focus tensions into specific actions (investigations, mob violence, and so forth) requires explanation. Billington provides this through scrutinizing the authenticity of claims by people such as Maria Monk and Rebecca Reed, reconstructing lines of communication and crossed paths of principal characters in the nativistic movement, and accounting for the effects of such propaganda pieces as <u>Awful Disclosures</u>.

It is obvious from this discussion that <u>Awful Disclosures</u> and <u>Origins of Nativism</u> are two vastly different types of historical accounts. Maria Monk's book, aside from the fact that the events it described were sheer fabrication and/or wildly embellished caricatures of convent life, had a political purpose that could as easily be served by fiction as by truth, if not better served by the former. This is a significant point to keep in mind since just as American culture continually provides fertile soil for unconventional religious groups to spring up, so it also breeds reactionary countermovements like the nativists which need (and one way or another will provide to the public) horrorific apostate accounts like Maria Monk's. Billington's book, conversely, serving no crusading ideological purpose, is true history, not simply because it attempts to ferret out real events from imaginary ones (which <u>Awful Disclosures</u> deliberately blurred) but also because it attempts to construct a larger meaning out of the feelings and events that <u>Awful Disclosure's</u> author(s) actually experienced but little understood reflectively.

NOTES

[1] Many of the ideas presented in this chapter have been developed elsewhere. On "anecdotal atrocity tales" and the defectors from religious groups who tell them, see Shupe and Bromley, 1980:150-64; Bromley and Shupe,

1979; and Bromley, Shupe and Ventimiglia, 1979.   I am
indebted also to my colleague Donna Oliver (see Oliver,
1980) who is developing a theory of apostasy in social
movements and who made critical bibliographic suggestions.

[2] There is little doubt that non-Irish and non-
Catholic Americans saw the United States as a specifically Protestant enterprise.   Says Marty (1970:15-6):
"Church people and the unchurched alike thought of the
new republic as a Protestant domain.   Geographies,
spellers, and readers from 1804, 1806, 1817, 1835, and
1846 included charts delineating the religions of the
nations of the world.   The United States was always
listed as Protestant."

[3] More complete listings of sources in the anti-
Catholic apostate literature can be found in Oliver
(1980) and Billington (1974, 1952).

REFERENCES

Billington, Ray Allen. 1974. The Origins of Nativism
      in the United States, 1800-1844. New York: Arno
      Press.

_____. 1952. The Protestant Crusade,
      1800-1860: A Study of the Origins of American Na-
      tivism. Gloucester, MA: Peter Smith.

_____. 1936-7. "Maria Monk and Her In-
      fluence." The Catholic Historical Review: 283-96.

Bromley, David G. and Anson D. Shupe, Jr. 1979. "The
      Tnevnoc Cult." Sociological Analysis 40 (Winter):
      361-66.

_____., Anson D. Shupe, Jr., and Joseph C.
      Ventimiglia. 1979. "The Role of Anecdotal Atroci-
      ties in the Social Construction of Evil." Paper

presented at the annual meeting of the American Sociological Association, Boston.

Davis, David Brion. 1960. "Some Themes of Counter-Subversion: An Analysis of Anti-Masonic, Anti-Catholic, and Anti-Mormon Literature." The Mississippi Valley Historical Review 47 (September): 205-224.

Edwards, Christopher. 1979. Crazy for God. Englewood Cliffs, NJ: Prentice-Hall.

Green, Nelson W., ed. 1857. Fifteen Years Among the Mormons: Being the Narrative of Mrs. Mary Ettie V. Smith. New York.

Gossett, Thomas F. 1965. Race: The History of an Idea in America. New York: Schocken.

Hopkins, Hiram. 1830. Renunciation of Free Masonry. Boston.

Martin, Rachel. 1979. Escape. Denver: Accent Books.

Marty, Martin E. 1970. Righteous Empire: The Protestant Experience in America. New York: Harper & Row.

Mills, Jeannie. 1979. Six Years With God. New York: A&W Publishers.

Monk, Maria. 1836. (reprinted in 1962). Awful Disclosures of the Hotel Dieu Nunnery. Handen: Anchor.

Morse, Samuel F.B. 1968. "The Dangers of Foreign Immigration." Pp. 158-63 in The Annals of America. Vol. 6: 1833-1840, The Challenge of a Continent. Chicago: William Benton.

Oliver, Donna L. 1980. "The Role of Apostates in the Mobilization of Counter-Movements." Unpublished Master's Thesis. The University of Texas at Arlington.

Olson, James Stuart. 1979. The Ethnic Dimension in American History. New York: St. Martin's Press.

Reed, Rebecca T. 1835 (reprinted). Six Months in a Convent. New York: Arno Press.

Thielmann, Bonnie. 1979. The Broken God. Elgin, IL: David C. Look.

Shannon, William V. 1966. The American Irish. (Revised edition) New York: The Macmillan Company.

Underwood, Barbara and Betty Underwood. 1979. Hostage to Heaven. New York: Clarkson N. Potter.

Ward, Maria. 1857. Female Life Among the Mormons: A Narrative of Many Years' Personal Experience, By the Wife of a Mormon Elder, Recently Returned from Utah. New York.

Wittke, Carl. 1970. The Irish in America. New York: Russell & Russell.

Wood, Allen Tate and J. Vitek. 1979. Moonstruck. New York: William Morrow.

Young, Ann Elizabeth. 1875. Wife No. 19: or, The Story of a Life in Bondage, Being a Complete Exposé of Mormonism. Hartford.

SUGGESTED FURTHER READING

Chaplin, J.P. 1959. Rumor, Fear, and the Madness of Crowds. New York: Ballantine Books.

Greeley, Andrew M. 1972. The Denominational Society. Glenview, IL: Scott, Foresman & Co.

Handlin, Oscar, ed. 1959. Immigration as a Factor in American History. Englewood Cliffs, NJ: Prentice-Hall.

Hansen, Marcus L. 1940. The Immigrant in American History. Cambridge, MA: Harvard University Press.

Herberg, Will. 1960. Protestant, Catholic, Jew. (Revised edition) Garden City, NY: Doubleday Anchor.

Shupe, Jr., Anson D. and David G. Bromley. 1981. "Apostates and Atrocity Stories: Some Parameters in the Dynamics of Deprogramming." In Bryan Wilson, ed., <u>The</u> <u>Social</u> <u>Impact</u> <u>of</u> <u>New</u> <u>Religious</u> <u>Movements</u>. New York: The Rose of Sharon Press, Inc.

THOUGHTS FOR FURTHER CONSIDERATION

In that late 1970s, as mentioned in this chapter, a number of ex-"cultists" (almost all former "Moonies", i.e., apostates from Sun Myung Moon's Unification Church) wrote books, published by perfectly respectable companies, that performed precisely the same function for the current anti-cult movement that Maria Monk's and Rebecca Reed's ghostwritten tracts performed for the nativist movement. Yet, unlike Monk and Reed who never belonged to the fringe group which their books attacked, most if not all of the current apostates were at one time bonafide members of a fringe religion. How is a modern historian to distinguish between those parts of their testimonies that are self-serving or merely spiced up to improve marketability and reader interest, and those segments that legitimately portray the questionable practices of a group? Ultimately, this question leads to another: to what extent is the comparison of the nineteenth century pseudo-apostates with twentieth century apostates appropriate?

CONCLUSION: THE TRUNK AND THE TAIL

There is a hoary Buddhist story about three blind
monks who, confronted with an elephant, tried to feel
and deduce what it was.   One felt the trunk. "It is a
snake-like being!" he concluded.   Another felt the elephant's underbelly. "It is enormous and round, like a
boulder!" the second exclaimed.   The third monk felt
one of the elephant's legs. "He is only several feet
in circumference, and in the shape of a tree stump,"
came the announcement.

Implicit in this anecdote is the assumption that
there really is an elephant that can be objectively and
reliably described, existing independently of its mistaken blind observers' theories.   In other words, to
make sense of the monks' descriptions we must assume
that there is a knowable, describable elephant to be
contrasted with their interpretations.   The humor comes
from the contrast between the monks' "social realities"
and the "material reality" of the beast, the knowledge
of which we share.

However, social phenomena often have no such clear-
cut referents for judging the accuracy, distortion or
misunderstanding of observers.   Hence there is no independent, material existence of an "elephant" that
exists alongside attempts to describe or imagine one.
Translated into terms of analyzing fringe religions,
this means that such groups are merely organizations

of like-minded people onto whom various types of scholars project their own disciplinary concerns. There is
no "cult", for example, with a meaning independent of
the person who studies it. Sociologist Donald Stone
(1978:142) compared the contemporary wave of fringe religions, onto which researchers project their own feelings and assumptions as "spiritual inkblots" and concluded that "reports of movements may tell us more about
the observers than about the observed." (1978:142) He
commented about the process of studying them:

> Knowledge about the new religious groups is
> situational. It is produced by the interac-
> tion of the researcher with the focus and ob-
> ject of study. It is always an interpreta-
> tion, influenced by the personal preferences,
> attitudes, and states of consciousness that
> the researchers (and reader) brings to the
> study. There are no immaculate perceptions.
> While bias is epistemologically inevitable,
> its influence on the interpretation can be
> gauged when it is made explicit. The greater
> the consciousness of possible bias, the great-
> er the certainty about the foundation on which
> our knowledge of these new religious movements
> rests.

This is the point to be remembered: THE SOCIAL
MEANINGS OF FRINGE RELIGIONS, UNLIKE THE INVARIATE PHYS-
ICAL MEANINGS OF PHYSICAL OBJECTS (SUCH AS ROCKS AND
ELECTRICAL CURRENTS), RESIDE IN THE MINDS OF OBSERVERS.
MEANING IS SOCIALLY CONSTRUCTED. THEREFORE THE VARIOUS
INTERPRETATIONS OF FRINGE RELIGIONS ARE BETTER UNDER-
STOOD AS ATTEMPTS TO CONSTRUCT COHERENT PHENOMENA WITH
REGULARITIES AND PREDICTABILITY RATHER THAN SIMPLY AS
ALTERNATIVE VIEWPOINTS OF ALREADY EXISTING PHENOMENA.

Fringe religions exist as conglomerates of human activity. That we, as outside observers, give them theological, psychological or social structural interpretations is our enterprise and not inherently theirs.

REFERENCES

Stone, Donald. 1978. "On Knowing How We Know About the New Religions." Pp. 141-52 in Jacob Needleman and George Baker, eds., Understanding the New Religions. New York: Seabury Press.